# The Birth of the Modern Mind: The Intellectual History of the 17th and 18th Centuries
## Parts I & II
### Alan Charles Kors, Ph.D.

**PUBLISHED BY:**

**THE TEACHING COMPANY**
**4151 Lafayette Center Drive, Suite 100**
**Chantilly, Virginia 20151-1232**
**1-800-TEACH-12**
**Fax—703-378-3819**
**www.teach12.com**

# Alan Charles Kors, Ph.D.

Professor of History, University of Pennsylvania

Alan Charles Kors received his bachelors degree from Princeton University and his masters and doctoral degrees from Harvard University. Since 1968, he has taught history at the University of Pennsylvania, where is now Professor of History, specializing in the intellectual history of Europe in the 17th and 18th centuries.

Professor Kors is the author and editor of several books on European intellectual history, including *D'Holbach's Coterie: An Enlightenment in Paris*; *Atheism in France, 1660-1729: The Orthodox Sources of Disbelief*; and *Anticipations of the Enlightenment in England, France, and Germany*. He has served as a member of the Council of the National Endowment for the Humanities and on the editorial boards of several scholarly journals. He has received postdoctoral fellowships from the American Council of Learned Societies, the Davis Center for Historical Studies at Princeton University, and the Smith Richardson Foundation. He is currently the editor-in-chief of the multi-volume Oxford University Press *Encyclopedia of the Enlightenment*.

Professor Kors has won two awards for distinguished college teaching and the Engalitcheff Award for defense of academic freedom. With Harvey A. Silverglate, he is coauthor of *The Shadow University: The Betrayal of Liberty on America's Campuses*, published in October 1998.

# Table of Contents
# The Birth of the Modern Mind:
## The Intellectual History of the 17<sup>th</sup> and 18<sup>th</sup> Centuries

# Table of Contents

## The Birth of the Modern Mind:
## The Intellectual History of the 17th and 18th Centuries

# The Birth of the Modern Mind:
# The Intellectual History of the 17<sup>th</sup> and 18<sup>th</sup> Centuries

## Scope:

When the 17<sup>th</sup> century dawned in Europe, the world of learning and formal understanding was dominated by a belief in the presumptive authority of those past authors who had stood the test of time and in the system of thought—Aristotelian scholasticism—that had emerged from the fusion of those authorities and Christian doctrine. A series of fundamental assaults upon the inherited intellectual system dominated the intellectual life of the 17<sup>th</sup> century, just as the combined effects of growth in education and printing dramatically expanded the size and opportunities of the reading public. Those assaults constituted nothing less than a conceptual revolution among students of natural philosophy (the study of natural things by the natural mind), a revolution that altered the European relationship to thought, nature, and human possibility. In the 18<sup>th</sup> century, that conceptual revolution—associated most clearly with what we now term the "scientific revolution," but which was a transformation of all aspects of human inquiry and understanding—was popularized, translated into new media, and extended to areas of nature and human activity beyond those imagined by most 17<sup>th</sup>-century thinkers. By the end of the 18<sup>th</sup> century, the prestige of ancient thought and of the inherited system was a thing of the past. Educated Europeans believed that they had a new understanding—of thought and the human mind, of method, of nature, and of the uses of knowledge—with which they could come to know the world correctly for the first time in human history and with which they could rewrite the possibilities of human life. The goal of these lectures is to understand that conceptual and cultural revolution as a historical phenomenon, seeing the birth of modern thought in the dilemmas, debates, and extraordinary works of the 17<sup>th</sup>- and 18<sup>th</sup>-century mind.

The broad themes of the 17<sup>th</sup> century's intellectual revolution involved a rejection of the presumptive authority of the past in general and a diverse set of furious assaults upon the inherited Aristotelian synthesis in particular. In the place of that authority and system, thinkers proposed systems and outlooks that sometimes reinforced each other (in ways that we often find odd today but that were understandable to 17<sup>th</sup>- and 18<sup>th</sup>-century readers) and that often competed with each other as possible replacements of the increasingly discredited authorities. These new systems and outlooks included empiricism, experimentalism, rationalism, quantification of nature, mechanism, skepticism about philosophy and certainty, and the radical separation of theology and natural inquiry. Readers often evaluated theories in purely abstract terms, but the public also came to see theories as tested or embodied in concrete works of inquiry. The most dramatic such example was Newton's *Principia Mathematica*, which so much of the culture came to believe had made the world comprehensible and coherent, and whose presumed system of inquiry became identified with the theory of knowledge advanced by John Locke in his *Essay Concerning Human Understanding*. The 18th century sought to take the models of Newton and Locke and apply them to the fullest possible range of human inquiry and endeavor.

The conceptual revolution of the 17th century was above all a series of philosophical clashes over abstract and fundamental issues, although its outcome was far from abstract. In the 18th century, the heirs of that conceptual revolution—the "new philosophers"—both popularized what they took to be the substance and implications of what had occurred in the 17th century and extended them to new areas of inquiry. They also dealt in various ways with the dramatic implications of the new philosophy for essential religious issues: miracle, revelation, supernaturalism, the authority of the priesthood, human nature, sin, and virtue. They sought to understand both society and religion in increasingly natural terms, to establish the rights of freedom of inquiry and belief, and to discredit, reform, or replace those authorities that could not justify themselves by the new criteria and proper uses of knowledge. In these endeavors, 18th-century thinkers effected a genuine cultural transformation more revolutionary than anything that occurred in the social or political life of 18th-century Europe. It would be false to attribute unintended consequences to the systems of thought from which these arose, but it is crucial to human understanding to know what have been, in fact, the consequences of ideas. This course will put us at the heart of the most far-reaching and consequential intellectual changes in the history of European civilization.

**Objectives:** Upon completion of this course, you should be able to:

1. Describe the major changes that occurred in the thought of the 17th and 18th centuries in terms of what the thinkers of this era most rejected in the intellectual inheritance with which this age began.

2. Summarize the main schools of 17th-century thought that influenced the cultural revolution of the 18th century.

3. Give an account of the revolution in epistemology (theories of knowledge) and ontology (theories of what exists as real) that most changed the ways in which European thought about their world.

4. Explain the so-called "scientific revolution" in terms of the debates and dilemmas of early modern thought.

5. Describe the problems posed by changes in thinking about nature and knowledge for the religious life of Europe.

6. Summarize which sides of 17th-century thinkers are appropriated and which sides are ignored by 18th-century thinkers.

7. Describe the conflicts that emerged in the 18th century between the "new philosophers" and the Church.

8. Explain how "the pursuit of happiness" became a compelling moral and political criterion for a religious culture.

9. Summarize the most striking unintended consequences of systems of thought in the 17th and 18th centuries.

10. Identify the most essential unresolved debates of the early modern period.

# Lecture One
# Introduction—Intellectual History and Conceptual Change

**Scope:** Although most generations and cultures view their own ways of thinking about the world as somehow "natural," ideas, including our most fundamental ways of thinking, change over time and have a particular history. Revolutions in ways of thinking are in many ways the most influential and far-reaching of all revolutions, because they affect our entire sense of legitimate authority, of the possible and the impossible, of right and wrong, and the potentials of human life. The revolution in thought that occurred in the 17th and 18th centuries was perhaps the most profound such transformation of European—if not human—life. Europe did nothing less than change its way of thinking about mind and knowledge themselves, about what is real in the world, and about how things happened. In short, Europe altered its relationship to knowledge and to nature. Political revolutions come and go, but this intellectual revolution has had enduring and profound effects. Our task is not to judge that revolution from various philosophical points of view, but to understand it as the 17th and 18th centuries understood it. Our goal is to observe and analyze the birth of the conceptual revolution of the 17th century and its popularization and extension in the cultural revolution of the 18th century.

**Objectives:** Upon completion of this lecture, you should be able to:

1. Explain why human beings cannot understand their history without understanding the history of their thought and conceptualizations.

2. Distinguish between the analytic or judgmental history of philosophy, on the one hand, and intellectual history, on the other.

3. Describe what is meant by an intellectual "revolution."

4. Distinguish between the conceptual revolution of the 17th century and the more general cultural revolution of the 18th century.

5. Explain the intensity of reading for the educated mind of early modern Europe.

# Outline

I. Abstract thought, as much or more than political, social, and economic behavior, has a history.

    **A.** Abstract thought (and, perhaps, a sense of the humorous) is a uniquely human characteristic.

        **1.** All higher species have relationships of power, social organization, and production. Human beings mediate all of those relationships by means of thought, which is why we have more than an evolutionary history.

        **2.** We change our thinking about the natural order—about what is out there (ontology, i.e., our speculation about kinds of existence and kinds of beings), why things happen (causality), and what knowledge itself is (epistemology).

    **B.** The history of our abstract thought is therefore an essential part of understanding ourselves as historical phenomena.

        **1.** Changes in our thinking and understanding alter our very relationship to nature (including to social phenomena).

        **2.** Every generation and civilization tends to think of its own way of thinking about the world (and about thinking itself) as somehow "natural." Intellectual history—the study of human intellectual behavior over time—teaches us, however, that our thought has a history, of which our way of thinking is the product. Learning that history, we see our own thought in relationship to its origins and to the often unintended consequences of those origins.

        **3.** If one were transported back to another time, one most easily would learn its relationships of power, production, social organization, and gender. The most foreign and difficult part of a past culture would be its way of thinking about the world and about thinking.

    **C.** Intellectual history is not the analytical or normative history of philosophy. Our goal is understanding the past as the past.

        **1.** The philosophical history of philosophy rightly asks about the truth value or power of prior ways of thought. Intellectual history explores the past in the spirit of the cultural anthropologist, not to judge of its merits or demerits, but to understand it, as much as is possible, on its own historical terms.

2. We shall not ask, therefore, who was wise or foolish but, rather, how the world looked from different perspectives, what debates and dilemmas produced what new ways of thinking, what emerged in the 17$^{th}$ and 18$^{th}$ centuries.

3. If we succeed, we should observe and understand more deeply nothing less than the birth of the modern mind.

II. The intellectual revolution of the 17$^{th}$ and 18$^{th}$ centuries was far more profound in its consequences for the human condition than any political or social revolution of the early modern period, and itself contributed crucially to revolutions in European life.

  A. If a culture changes the way it thinks about truth, nature, the knowable, the possible and impossible, and the causes of things, it will alter its expectations and behavior in almost all areas of human life.

  B. If a culture changes the way it thinks about using mind properly, it changes the way that it thinks about almost everything.

  C. A conceptual transformation is not confined to areas of thought alone. For example, to change one's evaluation of the force of inherited intellectual authority is to change one's whole attitude toward authority in general. To change one's attitude to the limits and possibilities of human life is to change one's expectations of and relationship to almost everything around one. This transformation occurs in the 17$^{th}$ and 18$^{th}$ centuries.

    1. The 17$^{th}$ century brought a conceptual revolution in often very abstract terms. It initiated a struggle for who shall be the teachers of a civilization and what will be the lessons taught.

    2. The 18$^{th}$ century brought a revolution in culture marked by the popularization of the conceptual revolution of the 17$^{th}$ century and by an extension of its consequences to new areas of human thought and activity.

    3. A telling example involves how we get to "the pursuit of happiness" as the very purpose of human society.

III. The culture of the early modern intellectual revolution was very different from our own.

  A. The subsistence economy of the time allowed only a few the necessary freedom from labor to study and think.

**B.** Travel was expensive and dangerous, and paintings were few. There were no media of mass communication to give one a window onto other times, places, and minds beyond one's provincial gaze.

**C.** Books brought with them an intense culture of close reading, logical argument, and pride in erudition and formal thought.

**D.** Our window onto the culture of that time is the texts that it produced, and the context in which those texts were written.

**Essential Reading:**

J.G.A. Pocock, *Politics, Language, and Time*, 1–41, 202–91.

**Supplementary Reading:**

Alan Charles Kors, *Atheism in France, 1650–1729: The Orthodox Sources of Disbelief*.

**Questions to Consider:**

1. What do we gain or lose by suspending judgment and seeking to understand the past on its own terms?

2. Why do most people not realize that they have an implicit philosophical system?

# Lecture Two
## The Dawn of the 17<sup>th</sup> Century—
## Aristotelian Scholasticism

**Scope:** Europe in the 17<sup>th</sup> century still had a traditionalist and subsistence culture. For that culture, past inheritances had a presumptive authority because they had stood the test of time and been successful parts of what had permitted mankind to survive. The term "innovator" was almost always a pejorative (usually preceded by the adjective "rash"). In the educated world, that intellectual inheritance was a fusion of Aristotelian (and other Greek) philosophy and of Christian theology; it was known as "scholasticism" or, more precisely, as Aristotelian scholasticism. Its means of teaching and persuasion was the *disputatio* (disputation), based upon (in order of importance) intellectual authorities, logical deduction from these authorities, and the appearances of the world. This system dominated the universities and schools of Europe. Thinkers believed that it brought coherence to the world, explaining the nature of all things in terms of their "material, formal, efficient, and final causes." By distinguishing among all beings in terms of the degrees of their "perfections," scholasticism created a "great chain of being" that permitted us to know contemplatively the value of all things. The science of final causes (teleology) permitted us to know contemplatively the purposes of things, and to grasp how, under God's design, all things strove for God's created order. The 17<sup>th</sup> century marked a momentous assault upon all aspects of the Aristotelian scholastic synthesis.

**Objectives:** Upon completion of this lecture, you should be able to:
1. Describe the authority of tradition in the pre-modern intellectual world.
2. Explain the *disputatio* (disputation).
3. Describe the Aristotelian use of "perfections" and "forms."
4. Summarize the Aristotelian system of causes.
5. Explain teleology.

**6.** Describe the implications of the "great chain of being" for the kinds of knowledge that were most valued.

**7.** Explain why an attack on Aristotle's method threatened the whole edifice of early modern learning.

## Outline

**I.** We begin with an overview of the intellectual inheritance of the 17th century.

    **A.** At the dawn of the 17th century, the dominant philosophical system was Aristotelian scholasticism—the philosophy of Aristotle as interpreted and adopted by the Christian schools of Europe.

    **B.** This system linked Aristotelian philosophy to Christian doctrine and provided the intellectual world of the 17th century with answers to fundamental questions such as: When should I be convinced? What should I find persuasive? When must I say, "Yes, I have to believe that?"

**II.** In Aristotelian scholasticism, philosophical arguments took the form of the *disputatio* (disputation). The *disputatio* emphasized three factors that compelled belief: authority, reason, and experience.

    **A.** Authority was either supernatural or natural.

        **1.** Supernatural authority was based on Scripture, as correctly understood by appropriate authorities.

        **2.** Natural authorities were based on the presumptive authority of the past (what had stood the test of time) —above all, the Greeks.

        **3.** The authority of ancient authors and texts was integrated into Christian theology and intellectual life, especially when the thought of those ancient authorities helped to explicate the truths of the Christian faith.

    **B.** Reason—and especially the principle of non-contradiction—was another source of belief.

        **1.** There are two modes of reason: inductive and deductive.

        **2.** The model appropriate to the practice of the early 17th century was deductive reason, by which one derived what follows logically from things known by authority.

      **C.** Experience was viewed not as the stuff of inductive logic, nor as a systematic means of inquiry, but instead as an illustration of things known by authority and logical deduction.

**III.** The Aristotelian system of causality gave the Western mind a sense of coherence, of knowing how and why things happen and what those things are.

      **A.** According to Aristotle, there are four components to the system of causality.

          **1.** The material cause is the stuff from which something is made (e.g., the marble of a marble statue).

          **2.** The formal cause is the particular form (e.g., the statue of Alexander the Great) realized from the stuff of the material cause (e.g., the marble).

          **3.** The efficient cause is what brings the form into actual existence from the matter (e.g., the sculptor with hammer and chisel).

          **4.** The final cause is the reason or purpose of the action (e.g., the end pursued by the sculptor). The science of final causes is "teleology."

      **B.** Operating principles allow us to distinguish among these causes.

          **1.** From distinctions among the essences brought into being in forms, we have a scale of perfections, at the top of which is God. We have a measure of the value and importance of everything.

          **2.** Thus, the immutable is higher and more important than the mutable.

          **3.** The goal of knowledge is the contemplative understanding of and appreciation of perfections and purposes.

**IV.** Aristotelian scholastic perspectives confer a distinct understanding of the world.

      **A.** Under God's design, all things strive for His order, for the fulfillment of His purposes.

      **B.** The world is a Great Chain of Being, a hierarchy of perfections. Given the mutable things of the earth and the immutable things of the heavens, there is a fundamental divide between sublunar and celestial beings and phenomena.

**C.** There is an essential hierarchy of "souls" governing "substantial forms."

    **1.** God is incorporeal and pure actuality.

    **2.** Angels are incorporeal and pure intellect, but unlike God they are imperfect.

    **3.** Man has a reasoning soul and a corporeal body; he is endowed with free will to choose between good and evil.

    **4.** Animals have an animal soul and physical senses. They have neither reason nor freedom of the will.

    **5.** Plants have a vegetative soul and undergo purposeful growth. They have no reproduction, no learning, and no choice.

    **6.** Stones are wholly body and lack soul and its behaviors.

**V.** Conclusion: The system and its consequences.

    **A.** In such a system, what should a mind capable of study know?

        **1.** It should have a deep knowledge of the system as a whole and its lessons.

        **2.** It should have knowledge of perfections and purposes, above all, contemplative classification yielding wisdom of God's creation and of our place in it. It should dwell on higher, not lower, things.

    **B.** This is the system that had emerged officially triumphant after all the intellectual wars of the Renaissance and the sixteenth century, enshrined in the official curricula of the secondary schools and universities of Western Europe.

    **C.** With Francis Bacon began the momentous assault on the predominance of this system of thought. Bacon sought:

        **1.** A reordering of the categories of the disputation.

        **2.** The overturning of the presumptive authority of the past.

        **3.** The separation of natural philosophy from theology.

**Essential Reading:**

Aristotle, *Metaphysics*, 1–39, 61–86, 169–199, 221–247.

**Supplementary Reading:**

Aristotle, *Physics.*

**Questions to Consider:**

1.  What would be the appeal of this Aristotelian system to Christian thinkers?

2.  How does the scholastic system encourage or discourage certain kinds of inquiry?

©1998 The Teaching Company.

# Lecture Three
# The New Vision of Francis Bacon

**Scope:** From the end of the sixteenth century until his death, the politician and philosopher Francis Bacon (1561–1626) undertook to criticize the Western intellectual inheritance, to transform the human quest for knowledge, and to put knowledge at the service of gaining power over the forces of nature upon which our suffering or well-being depended. For Bacon, the many causes of error (the Idols of the Mind) hindered us from understanding the world as created by God. The key to overcoming error was correct method, which for Bacon meant induction from the particulars of nature to general principles that could be tested experimentally. Nature, not the errant mind, should determine the truth or falsity of our beliefs. Unable to refute Aristotelianism on its own terms, he appealed to the charity and power inherent in his model and his redefinition of knowledge, and he highlighted the advantages that would accrue to both faith and natural philosophy if each were restricted to its proper sphere. His most essential work, *The New Organon*, argued that such an inductive, experimental science, free from the dead weight of the past, could yield a new kind of knowledge that would be dynamic, cumulative, and useful. His ultimate vision was that human beings, if governed by charity, could use knowledge to alter their relationship to nature and society on behalf of "the effecting of all things possible."

**Objectives:** Upon completion of this lecture, you should be able to:

1. Explain Bacon's dissatisfaction with the Aristotelian system and the European philosophical inheritance.

2. Summarize Bacon's theory of error, the "Idols of the Mind."

3. Describe Bacon's goals for human knowledge.

4. Explain the importance of "method" to Bacon's vision.

5. Explain why Bacon saw his philosophy as more pious than that of the scholastics.

6. Summarize the four essential themes of Bacon's *New Organon.*

# Outline

I. Bacon was dissatisfied with the Aristotelian scholastic orthodoxy that reigned in the universities of 16$^{th}$-century Europe.

    **A.** Bacon's life reflected the changes occurring in the audience of higher education. He entered Cambridge University at the end of the sixteenth century, encountering the traditional Aristotelian education but brimming with worldly ambitions and concerns.

    **B.** A contemporary wrote that it was at Cambridge that Bacon "first fell into the dislike of the philosophy of Aristotle … being a philosophy only strong for disputations and contentions, but barren of the production of works for the benefit of mankind."

    **C.** Bacon argued that the European philosophical tradition stood condemned on two main grounds.
        **1.** It had mixed religion and natural philosophy, to the confusion of both.
        **2.** It had substituted concern for words in place of concern for things.

    **D.** For Bacon, European thought had become enslaved to the systems of five or six Greeks. These systems had infected Europe's relationship with nature.

II. Bacon sought in two fundamental ways to win readers to his redefinition of the goals of human knowledge.

    **A.** New kinds and methods of knowledge would make possible an expansion of human empire over the phenomena on which our suffering or well-being depend.

    **B.** The Christian ethic entails knowledge in the service of charity, which means that the fruits of knowledge must permit one to enhance the condition of one's fellow creatures.

III. Bacon's *New Organon*—his new instrument or method for acquiring useful knowledge—was his most essential work. In it he set forth his "Great Instauration."

    **A.** The *New Organon* had four essential and profoundly influential themes.
        **1.** Knowledge is human power.
        **2.** Natural philosophy (science) is separate from theology.

3. Scientific knowledge requires the method of induction, from particulars to generalizations, always tested by experiment and open to revision.

4. Science is a dynamic, cooperative, and cumulative enterprise.

**B.** Bacon cautioned Christians against worshiping false "Idols of the Mind" rather than God's actual creations.

1. Idols of the Tribe are sources of error inherent in human nature.

2. Idols of the Cave are the particular biases of individual men.

3. Idols of the Marketplace result from the ambiguity of words.

4. Idols of the Theatre are our received philosophical tradition, worshipped under the notion of authority, especially that of Aristotle.

**IV.** In the *New Atlantis,* Bacon examined the place of natural knowledge in society.

**A.** In Bacon's utopian vision, all human beings would govern their relationship to nature and society on behalf of their own interest in human well-being.

**B.** The instrument of mankind's betterment was knowledge methodically drawn from patient observation and experiment, "to the [end of] effecting of all things possible."

**Essential Reading:**

Francis Bacon, *Novum Organum* (*The New Organon*), Introduction and Book One.

**Supplementary Reading:**

Francis Bacon, *The New Atlantis.*

**Questions to Consider:**

1. Why, for Bacon, is fundamental philosophy so essential to charity?

2. When later scientists, including Newton, described themselves as "Baconian," what parts of his system did they in fact take or not take as their own?

# Lecture Four
# The New Astronomy and Cosmology

**Scope:** Astronomy—the study of the immutable heavens—was an eminent science in the 17th century, and it is not accidental that so much of the challenge to scholasticism began in that field of inquiry. The astronomy adopted by the Aristotelian scholastics was that of Claudius Ptolemy (second century A.D.), which fit wonderfully with their system. Among the challenges to Aristotelianism in the early modern era was neo-Pythagorean thought, which viewed the universe in terms of mathematics and geometry, not in terms of Aristotelian "qualities," and which saw the sun as an emblem of God's divinity. Copernicus in the sixteenth century, and Johannes Kepler (1571–1630) in the 17th century, sought to create a more harmonious view of the heavens by placing the sun at the center of the system. Kepler, driven by neo-Pythagorean passions and possessing better data about the heavenly bodies than his predecessors had, devised his three laws of planetary motion which he believed disclosed God's mathematical order in the universe. Galileo (1564–1642) did not accept Kepler's laws (which would not be proven until Newton), but he did polemicize for the heliocentric astronomy and for a quantitative rather than qualitative view of nature. He castigated the scholastics for adhering blindly to human books rather than inquiring into God's book of nature; he criticized the use of Scripture as a scientific textbook; and he urged observation, reason, mathematical proofs, and attention to the quantities of nature as the means to know God's creation. Kepler and Galileo exemplified the great enthusiasm that 17th-century thinkers felt upon believing that they, for the first time, were observing and understanding God's actual work.

**Objectives:** Upon completion of this lecture you should be able to:

1. Describe the appeal of the Ptolemaic astronomy to the scholastics.

2. Summarize the essential features of the neo-Pythagorean challenge to Aristotelian thought.

3. Explain why Kepler's metaphysical commitments must be taken into account in order to explain his astronomy.

4. Describe Kepler's own sense of his accomplishment.

5. Distinguish between primary and secondary qualities in Galileo's system.

6. Explain the implications of the quantitative philosophy for Aristotelian conceptions.

7. Describe Galileo's sense of why Scripture could not be used to contradict the truths of natural philosophy.

# Outline

I. The Aristotelian scholastics had adopted the astronomy of the Greek astronomer Ptolemy.

A. Ptolemaic astronomy seemed wonderfully consistent with the scholastics' philosophical and theological systems.

B. It held that the earth was at the center of the universe. The moon, planets, sun, and an orb of fixed starts revolved around the earth in perfect circular motion.

II. Among the intellectual movements that arose to challenge Aristotelian scholasticism was neo-Pythagorean thought. Where the scholastics viewed God's creation in terms of perfections and purposes, the neo-Pythagoreans viewed it in terms of mathematics and geometry.

A. The worldview of Aristotelian scholasticism was qualitative, not quantitative, in its conception of the universe and of natural phenomena. It was essentialistic and teleological in its view of motion.

B. For the neo-Pythagoreans, the mind of God expressed itself in the order, harmonies, and ratios of the creation. Reality emanated from the Divinity itself and was numerical and geometrical.

C. Neo-Pythagoreans saw the sun—a luminous, perfect circle—as an emblem of the Divinity.

III. The work of Johannes Kepler reveals both the fusion of neo-Pythagorean numbers mysticism and natural philosophy on the one hand, and the fruitfulness of a quantitative science on the other.

A. Copernicus advanced an unproven heliocentric hypothesis.

**B.** Kepler believed that with the sun at the rightful center of the universe, the quantitative and geometrical harmonies and ratios of God's creation would be disclosed.

**C.** After going through an ordeal of mathematical hard labor, Kepler arrived at his first two laws of planetary motion.

    **1.** His first law held that the planets, including the earth, described elliptic, not circular, orbits around the sun.

    **2.** His second law held that the line joining a planet to the sun—the radial vector—sweeps out equal areas in equal times.

**D.** Kepler loathed the "imperfect" ellipses.

    **1.** For ten more years, he engaged in a computational struggle to find God's harmony in this universe of ellipses.

    **2.** In 1619, he found it in his third law of planetary motion: the square of the period of revolution of a planet is proportional to the cube of its average distance from the sun.

**IV.** Like Kepler, Galileo viewed reality in quantitative terms.

**A.** Although Galileo rejected Kepler's laws as too speculative, he shared Kepler's sense that nature was to be understood quantitatively and not in terms of perfections or purposes.

**B.** Galileo's most revolutionary assault upon Aristotelian scholasticism was not his Copernican astronomy, but his rejection of qualitative perfections and his distinction between secondary and primary qualities.

    **1.** Secondary qualities, in which category he placed almost all of the Aristotelian qualities, were not real in the objects thus described, but depended upon human perception (e.g. sweetness, color, immutability).

    **2.** Primary qualities defined what truly existed apart from perception, the qualities of objects themselves, the reality of God's natural creation. These were all quantitative: dimension, shape, the measurable.

    **3.** "Perfections" were human projections upon a natural world that was quantity in motion, a world to be understood in terms of mathematical law.

    **4.** Empirical observation, mathematical ordering, and mathematical test lead to laws of motion. Motion describes the relationship of bodies to time and distance; it does not express the perfections or purposes of things.

**V.** Galileo struggled with the Aristotelians.

    **A.** Galileo argues explicitly against Aristotle and against the principle of intellectual authority. He reminded scholastics of Aristotle's commitment to induction: "If Aristotle were here today, he would agree with me."

    **B.** In response to critics of the new astronomy who insisted that Copernican hypotheses were contradicted by Scripture, Galileo distinguished between the two revelations from God: His book of nature (our source of knowledge about the creation) and His book of Scripture (our source of knowledge about salvation and things beyond nature).

    **C.** For Galileo, our senses, intellect, reason, and mathematical proofs are from God. Experience and mathematical logic are irrefutable because God's creation is the ultimate test.

    **D.** Rejecting authority, 17th-century authors believed that for the first time, with proper method, the human mind was looking upon God's work with understanding.

**Essential Reading:**

Stillman Drake, ed., *The Discoveries and Opinions of Galileo,* 1–20, 58–85, 104–119, 173–216, 229–280.

**Supplementary Reading:**

Galileo, *Dialogue Concerning the Two Chief World Systems.*

**Questions to Consider:**

1. Modern scientists often believe that 17th-century scientists were practical experimentalists just like themselves. How different are Kepler and Galileo from modern scientists in their thought and work?

2. Why is astronomy such a dramatic field for anti-Aristotelian thought?

# Lecture Five
# Descartes's Dream of Perfect Knowledge

**Scope:** From (at least) the time of Plato, it has been a dream of Western philosophy to know things as they truly are, in and of themselves, undistorted by the human senses, passions, and perspective. In the 17th century, Descartes embodied that dream. He created a coherent philosophical system that posed, on the Continent, the major challenge to the scholastic hegemony, arousing great enthusiasms and projects. Descartes sought to demonstrate that we could establish a criterion of truth, and, with it, know with certainty the real nature and the real causes of things. For his legions of disciples, Descartes's work accomplished this and more: it freed philosophy from authority and from the Aristotelians; it explained the nature of ideas, knowledge, and the source of error; it refuted the skeptics who denied the possibility of certainty; it proved the existence of God and the immortality of the soul; it demonstrated that the physical world was matter in motion according to the laws of mechanics, making possible a rigorous new quantitative science of all physical reality; and it established the absolute distinction between body and mind—that is, between matter and spirit. In all of these things, it challenged scholasticism in the most fundamental ways and altered the nature and problems of Western philosophy and science.

**Objectives:** Upon completion of this lecture, you should be able to:

1. Explain why Descartes could appeal simultaneously to physicists and mystical theologians.

2. Describe how Descartes seeks to overcome "hyperbolic doubt" and establish a criterion of certainty.

3. Summarize Descartes's two proofs of God.

4. Explain Descartes's theory of extension and its implications for explaining nature.

5. Describe the nature of Cartesian dualism.

# Outline

I.   René Descartes sought to reconstruct all of human knowledge. His Cartesian philosophy posed the greatest challenge to Aristotelian scholasticism during the 17$^{th}$ century, above all on the Continent.

    **A.**  The ultimate vision of Western philosophy was encapsulated in Plato's image of the cave (knowing things in themselves, as they really are).

    **B.**  Descartes's dream was to attain perfect knowledge of being and of causes.

    **C.**  Descartes appealed to both mechanistic scientists and mystical theologians.

II.  Why does a thinker come to define the options of an intellectual age?

    **A.**  Many things vital or troubling to the period converged in Descartes's work.

    **B.**  Cartesian philosophy responded to five principal problems.

        **1.**  The first was the epistemological crisis brought about by the Reformation.

        **2.**  The second was the revival and appeal of classical skepticism during the 16$^{th}$ century.

        **3.**  The third was the specter of libertinism and the new Pyrrhonism.

        **4.**  The fourth was the neo-Pythagorean revival.

        **5.**  The fifth was the assault on Aristotle.

III. Descartes's *Meditations* described his quest for certainty.

    **A.**  He applied hyperbolic doubt; he propounded a skepticism that went beyond that of the skeptics and their critics.

    **B.**  Descartes offered a single indubitable proposition: "*cogito ergo sum.*" His criteria of the truth of ideas were clarity and distinctness.

    **C.**  Descartes had to show that his system could prove the existence of God. He offered two proofs that he regarded as self-evident and indubitable.

        **1.**  Every idea has an object that is its cause. The idea of an infinitely perfect God can come only from a perfect Being.

      **2.** Existence is a necessary property of God as a perfect Being.

    **D.** We know that an external reality corresponds to our ideas because God is not a deceiver.

**IV.** Descartes's physics caused at least as much intellectual excitement as did his metaphysics.

    **A.** Descartes' distinction between the essences of soul and body leads to Cartesian dualism: immaterial soul and material body.

    **B.** The essence of soul is thought; the essence of body is extension in height, width, and breadth.

    **C.** What can be known about extension? Descartes reached basically the same conclusion reached by Galileo: the physical world is dimension, motion, and the mechanisms of matter touching and communicating force to matter.

    **D.** Given God's will, nature operates according to fixed mechanical laws of motion, from which Descartes deduces inertia. The task of a new science is to discover the laws, mechanisms, and effects of matter in motion.

**V.** Four elements constitute the Cartesian legacy.

    **A.** Dualism: we inhabit a universe composed of two distinct substances—mind and matter.

    **B.** All matter is governed by natural mechanisms that science must understand.

    **C.** The mind-body problem: according to Cartesian philosophy, the two substances should not interact, but in fact they do. This problem will haunt Descartes, his followers, and Western philosophy.

    **D.** Cartesians reject all beliefs, such as superstition and witchcraft belief, holding that matter is affected by immaterial forces.

**VI.** Conclusion.

    **A.** Descartes's philosophy raised important problems: how to explain the interaction of spirit and matter in human life; the Eucharist; and the concept of miracle?

    **B.** The implications for authority, Aristotle, and natural knowledge are dramatic. Descartes holds that all knowledge begins with radical doubt.

**C.** Descartes leaves his followers with the great dream of perfect knowledge (complete and evident).

**Essential Reading:**

René Descartes, *Meditations on First Philosophy*.

———, *The Passions of the Soul*.

**Supplementary Reading:**

René Descartes, *Discourse on Method.*

**Questions to Consider:**

1. In the final analysis, does Descartes's system strengthen or weaken the relationship between theological and scientific questions?

2. The debate between Cartesians and Aristotelians will dominate 17th-century intellectual life. What are the issues that most separate them?

# Lecture Six
# The Specter of Thomas Hobbes

**Scope:** Thomas Hobbes (1588–1679) attracted few disciples, but the force and threat of his philosophical arguments set much of the debate in the century that followed him. He brought together sensationalistic empiricism, deterministic mechanism, materialism, and ethical relativism into one powerful philosophical alternative to scholasticism and Cartesianism. Rejecting Descartes's dualism of mind and body, Hobbes argued that we only can conceive and know of material things, and that all language of immateriality is nonsensical and insignificant. The world, including the entire realm of human experience, was matter in motion according to fixed, mechanical laws. There was no freedom of the will, and all things were the necessary results of prior causes. Human beings were governed by the pursuit of pleasure and the flight from pain (ego-psychology), which had produced a condition in which life was "nasty, poor, solitary, brutish, and short." The great task of both philosophy and the state was to save us from such an unwanted condition. Philosophy could do this by giving us real knowledge of the actual causes of our well-being and suffering and a real understanding of how to alter the world.

**Objectives:** Upon completion of this lecture, you should be able to:

1. Explain how a thinker without many disciples could be quite influential.

2. Describe Hobbes's view of the goal of philosophy.

3. Explain Hobbes's rejection of Cartesian dualism.

4. Summarize Hobbes's sense of why a sensationalistic empiricism leads to a materialistic philosophy.

5. Give an account of Hobbes's view of human nature.

6. Explain what Hobbes means by "good" and "evil."

# Outline

**I.** Hobbes's philosophy haunted the second half of the 17th and the first half of the 18th centuries. Even without many followers, Hobbes set the terms of many debates.

    **A.** Formal thought did not abandon the field to Hobbes. It became the test of a system of philosophy to appear to overcome the problems posed by Hobbes.

    **B.** It became useful to philosophers to brand their opponents as "Hobbists," and to find similarities between Hobbes and their rivals.

    **C.** Hobbes became, in effect, a set of objections and a set of unacceptable conclusions.

**II.** While Hobbes is most widely read today for his political philosophy, his theories of knowledge, language, being, and ethics set the early modern world on edge.

    **A.** The political doctrines of *Leviathan* follow from his general philosophy, and they can only be understood in that context.

    **B.** According to Hobbes, the goals of both philosophy and the state are survival and civil peace.

**III.** Hobbes's metaphysics is based on empiricism, materialism, and determinism.

    **A.** Hobbes's objection to Descartes: " I think, therefore matter is capable of thought."

    **B.** We can conceive only of corporeal (material) entities and their behaviors, and our language and our ontology (theory of being) must follow from that knowledge.

    **C.** Epistemology (theory of knowledge) produces a coherent materialist ontological language.

        **1.** All ideas enter the mind through the senses, which are physical.

        **2.** What affects the physical senses does so through physical contact, and thus it must be physical.

        **3.** Thus all coherent ideas are caused by bodies and their actions affecting the five senses.

    **D.** Materialism is the only alternative to speaking nonsense.

1. Words are signs or marks that represent physically caused sensory impressions.
2. A word without a material sensory referent is a "mere sound," "nonsense" (literally and figuratively), whatever emotions it evokes in us. It signifies nothing and thus is "insignificant speech."
3. Notions such as "soul," "ghost," or "immaterial being" either are metaphors for material entities or they are gibberish.
4. Thus there is no understanding of God. Reverence of the incomprehensible is an appropriate religious response.

E. Hobbes holds to deterministic mechanism.
1. Number and geometry, which are fixed and necessary relationships, govern quantitative relations, and all matter exists as quantity and shape.
2. Thus, the laws of nature are both mechanistic and determined. There is no uncaused event, and there is no "chance."

IV. Hobbes's philosophy of man rests upon materialism and ethical relativism.

A. Materialist and mechanistic determinism extends to human life.
1. The brain is a physical agent governed by the laws of nature.
2. What we experience as free will is in fact a profit-loss calculation.

B. Pleasure and pain: ego-psychology is the cause of human action.
1. All organisms seek pleasure and feel pain (or, more precisely, seek what they believe will cause pleasure and flee what they believe will cause pain).
2. Without the threat of punishment for harming others, this drive to pleasure produces "the war of all against all," in which life is "nasty, poor, solitary, brutish, and short."
3. Given the unbearability of that condition, we seek knowledge and social relations that will reduce our danger and enhance our well-being.
4. Again, this is the goal both of philosophy and of the state.

C. Good and evil: ego-psychology is the cause of relativistic human ethics.
1. All that we mean by "good" is that which we deem conducive to our happiness.

    **2.** All that we mean by "evil" is that which we deem conducive to our suffering.

    **3.** Thus there is no goodness or evil in and of themselves, but only in relationship to the human condition.

  **D.** This honest knowledge of ourselves and our natural condition can lead to the improvement of the human condition.

## Essential Reading:

Thomas Hobbes, *Leviathan*, Books I, II, and IV.

## Supplementary Reading:

Thomas Hobbes, *Metaphysical Writings*, 1–41, 52–80, 113–162.

## Questions to Consider:

**1.** May one read Hobbes as a religious believer, or must one "translate" his religious references into his materialism?

**2.** Is Hobbes merely talking about epistemology (what we may know), or is he as much of an ontological realist (with a theory about the real nature of being) as Descartes?

# Lecture Seven
# Skepticism and Jansenism—Blaise Pascal

**Scope**: Philosophical skepticism is the belief that we may know nothing with certainty. When it is used to humble human reason and demonstrate our dependence upon religious faith, it was termed "fideism." In the 17th century, fideism is yet another systematic assault on the dominant Aristotelian scholasticism. One of the two most influential fideists (the other, Pierre Bayle, is the subject of a later lecture) was Blaise Pascal (1623–1662), who abandoned a brilliant career in mathematics and the physical sciences to devote himself to piety and religious polemics. Pascal was a member of the Jansenist movement within French Catholicism, which stressed an Augustinian view of the catastrophic effects of the Fall upon the human will. Jansenism argued for the need for salvation by faith alone, a state achievable only by God's grace. Pascal's *Pensées*, his unfinished thoughts on religion, became one of the publishing sensations of the 17th century. It stressed the misery and absurdity of man and human life without God, the insufficiency of intellectual knowledge of God (especially without Christ), and the role of grace and the heart in faith. In the light of such faith, Pascal found that what seemed incoherent and self-contradictory about the world fell into place, like certain paintings looked at from the appropriate perspective.

**Objectives:** Upon completion of this lecture, you should be able to:

1. Explain the concept of "fideism."
2. Summarize the essential views of Jansenism on sin and salvation.
3. Explain what Pascal means by the "contradictions" and "misery" of human life.
4. Distinguish Pascal's "wager" from a "proof" of God.
5. Describe Pascal's view of faith and its effects.

# Outline

I. Skepticism is another systematic philosophical assault upon the dominance of Aristotelian scholastic thought.

**A.** There are deep skeptical strains in the 17th century about the claims of human knowledge.

**B.** Fideism was the dominant form of 17th-century skepticism.
  1. It held that human knowledge cannot attain significant certainty.
  2. It held that this weakness should convince us of our dependence upon faith and grace.

**C.** Two influential models of 17th-century fideism were provided by the Catholic Blaise Pascal and the Protestant Pierre Bayle.

**II.** Pascal and Jansenism.

**A.** Pascal was a child prodigy in mathematics, and he began a brilliant scientific career. He did ground-breaking work on conic sections, cycloid curves, barometrics, fluid dynamics, pneumatics, and the mathematical calculus of probability.

**B.** He abandoned his scientific career following his encounter with Jansenism, which expressed the age-old contest between piety and natural knowledge.

**C.** Within Catholicism, Jansenism was a continuation of the contest between Augustinianism and Thomism.
  1. Jansenism emphasized the catastrophic effects of the Fall upon will and reason.
  2. It stressed the absolute dependence of all human beings on God's grace, which comes through a personal encounter with Christ rather than through the sacraments.
  3. Antoine Arnauld decried the scandal of frequent communion.

**D.** Jansenism became the religious and political underground of France. The Jansenist convent at Port Royal was a center of moral and ecclesiastical revolt.

**E.** Pascal became one of the foremost apologists of Jansenism, Catholicism, and Christianity.

**III.** Pascal's unfinished work of Christian apologetics—The *Pensées*—was edited and arranged by his Jansenist friends at Port-Royal.

**A.** The *Pensées*—Pascal's thoughts on religion—electrified his own and later generations.

**B.** The *Pensées* stressed the following themes.

1. Pascal stresses man's misery without God, and his avoidance of the deepest question: Who am I, and what is my fate?
2. He laments the simultaneous realism and absurdity of the human condition (e.g., hatred and war; symbolism and power).
3. Mankind is a mass of inexplicable contradictions (e.g., genius and ignorance, science without morality, energy without purpose, reason and arbitrary custom).
4. We are creatures of intellectual weakness. We use reason without sincerity, we are swayed by passions and prejudices, and we cannot grasp the infinitely large or the infinitesimally small.
5. Pascal's "wager" is intended to incite the listener to believe in God. Knowing all of the above, and given the stakes, we should wish for the deepest answers, for the eternal, and for the existence of God.
6. Knowledge of God, however, is insufficient without knowledge of Christ.
7. One believes by means of one's heart, if it has been touched by grace. The heart has reasons that reason cannot understand.
8. With faith, our contradictions and unhappiness, our greatness and depravity, all fall into place.
9. Inner peace and salvation are the goals of life.

## Essential Reading:

Blaise Pascal, *Pensées* (*Thoughts on Religion*).

## Supplementary Reading:

Blaise Pascal, *Provincial Letters.*

## Questions to Consider:

1. Why would many theologians, as they did, find Pascal's fideism, for all of its piety, dangerous to religion?
2. Is Pascal appealing to a religious (and moral) experience that is as much "data" about the world as are the objects of Bacon's, Galileo's, or Descartes's inquiries?

# Lecture Eight
# Newton's Discovery

**Scope**: Isaac Newton played a magisterial role in the intellectual and scientific revolutions of the 17th century, but he was a product and culmination of those phenomena. Inspired by Bacon, Descartes's mathematics, and the progress of experimental and mechanistic science, many anti-Aristotelian intellectuals were in communication with each other by the mid-17th century. In England there emerged the Royal Society, which conducted experiments and observations, presented reports, and published *Transactions*, vastly enlarging the participants in and the audience of the new experimental science. It was also the first to publish Newton's scientific work. Shortly after receiving his bachelor's degree at Cambridge, Newton—in one eighteen-month stretch—formulated the law of gravity, laid the foundations of modern physics in his laws of motion, transformed the entire science of optics, and created the calculus. Not until two decades later, however, was his work on physics and astronomy communicated to the world. The great astronomer Edmund Halley saw at once the scope of Newton's accomplishments and underwrote the publication in 1687 of Newton's *Philosophiae Naturalis Principia Mathematica*—the Mathematical Principles of Natural Philosophy.

**Objectives:** Upon completion of this lecture, you should be able to:

1. Explain the significance of the growth of scientific academies and societies outside of the universities.

2. Describe the emergence and composition of the Royal Society.

3. Explain the importance of Cartesianism to Newton's intellectual formation.

4. Summarize the accomplishments of Newton during his eighteen months at Woolesthorpe.

5. Explain why Edmund Halley was so astonished and exhilarated by Newton's papers on universal gravitation.

# Outline

**I.** Introduction: The emergence of Isaac Newton.

    **A.** Europe in the mid-17$^{th}$ century witnesses the growth, apart from universities, of societies of mathematically and mechanistically oriented empirical natural philosophy.

        **1.** The universities continued to be dominated by Aristotelian physics.

        **2.** Those drawn to new ways of thinking founded new institutions outside of academia.

    **B.** Beginning in the 1640s, intellectuals met in England to discuss non-Aristotelian natural philosophy. A generation arose that was excited by the work of Bacon and the progress of the mechanistic sciences.

    **C.** Bacon's work gave profound inspiration to later generations of scientists.

**II.** The Royal Society patronized the new philosophy and especially the work of Isaac Newton.

    **A.** The Royal Society was devoted to "physico-mathematico-experimental reasoning." It conducted experiments, presented reports, and published transactions, which were eagerly awaited by the public.

    **B.** It was chartered in 1662 by Charles II.

    **C.** In 1664 the Royal Society divided into eight committees: mechanical, astronomical and optical, anatomical, chemical, agricultural, history of trade, recording of hitherto unobserved or unrecorded phenomena, and correspondence.

    **D.** Bacon's *New Atlantis* defined the self-image of the Royal Society.

    **E.** The publication of Isaac Newton's "Optics" in the *Transactions* of the Royal Society was a major event in the history of Western science.

**III.** The scientific career of Isaac Newton.

    **A.** Newton entered Trinity College, Cambridge University in 1661. Unlike the rest of the university, which was dominated by Aristotelians, Trinity College was a Cartesian stronghold.

**B.** Newton was introduced to Cartesian thought and to higher mathematics.

**C.** Shortly after receiving his degree, Newton spent an unparalleled eighteen months in the countryside to avoid the plague, during which time he altered the history of the world.

    **1.** He discovered the law of gravity, which allowed him to explain inertial circular motion.

    **2.** He posited the three essential laws of mechanics that would govern Western physics.

    **3.** He invented the infinitesimal calculus.

    **4.** He founded modern optics (the science of light) with his experimental discovery of the composition of light.

**D.** In 1684, the magnitude of Newton's accomplishments was revealed when he was invited to contribute his views to a gathering of the great scientific minds of the time: Edmund Halley, Sir Christopher Wren, and Robert Hooke.

    **1.** Newton astonished them with his mathematical proof of the law of gravitation.

    **2.** At Halley's urging and expense, Newton further developed his general system of the laws of motion, which he published in 1687 as the *Philosophiae Naturalis Principia Mathematica*, better known simply as the *Principia.*

**Essential Reading:**

Alexandre Koyre, *Newtonian Studies.*

**Supplementary Reading:**

Alexandre Koyre, *Metaphysics and Measurement.*

**Questions to Consider:**

**1.** What does it tell us that the new experimental natural philosophy is finding a home apart from the universities?

**2.** Are Newton's extraordinary accomplishments in his eighteen months at Woolesthorpe indicative of anything in the culture beyond the prodigious brilliance of Isaac Newton?

# Lecture Nine
# The Newtonian Revolution

**Scope:**   The publication of Newton's *Principia* was not merely a major event in the history of Western science, but a watershed in the history of Western culture. A mathematical demonstration of the Copernican hypothesis as proposed by Kepler, the *Principia* convinced the majority of its readers (and the readers of those who popularized and explained it) that the world was ordered and coherent, and that the human mind, using Baconian method and mathematical reasoning, could understand that order. The enthusiasm for Newton, based often on the success of his predictions, extended far beyond those who could understand his work. The Newtonian triumph, however, was not immediate. The work was opposed by the Cartesians, whose physics had itself triumphed over the Aristotelians. To the Cartesians, Newton's description of occult action at a distance (gravity) violated the clarity and logic of mechanistic explanation. Cartesian-Newtonian debate went to the heart of what we mean by scientific explanation, and it raised vital issues of theology as well. Newton at first had sought a mechanistic explanation of gravity, but he made a virtue out of necessity by insisting that science should not feign hypotheses, that it should be limited in its ultimate claims. Newton (and the Newtonians) also believed that natural philosophy proved the existence of God (and His omnipotence) from the order and contingency of the world. The Newtonian synthesis gave to the culture a great confidence in inductive science, the mathematization of motion, and natural theology.

**Objectives:** Upon completion of this lecture, you should be able to:

1. Explain why Kepler's laws of planetary motion were not proven until Newton's *Principia.*

2. Describe the enthusiastic reception of Newton's work by the learned world.

3. Explain why the Cartesians saw Newton's gravitational force as a return to the occult forces and mysterious explanations of the Aristotelians.

4. Summarize Newton's conclusions about scientific explanation.

**5.** Explain the religious issues raised and addressed by Newton.

**6.** Summarize Newton's non-scientific legacy to early-modern culture.

# Outline

**I.** The publication of Newton's *Principia* was a watershed in the history of science and culture.

 **A.** Newton's *Principia* was a mathematical demonstration of the Copernican hypothesis as proposed by Kepler.

 **B.** It also convinced the culture that the world was ordered and lucid and that the human mind was capable of understanding the architecture and design of God in the creation.

 **C.** Newton's work generated great enthusiasm; his predictions convinced even those who could not understand the arguments.

  **1.** Edmund Halley said of Newton, "Nearer the gods no mortal may approach."

  **2.** In the words of Alexander Pope: "Nature and nature's laws lay hid in night. God said, 'Let Newton be,' and all was light."

**II.** Newtonians versus Cartesians.

 **A.** Cartesians explained the physical world in terms of matter contacting matter.

 **B.** Newtonian gravity—and the phenomenon of action at a distance— appeared to the Cartesians as a quasi-Aristotelian occult force.

 **C.** Newton and his followers made a virtue out of a necessity. They explained *that* a certain force operates, not *why* or *how*.

 **D.** Science should not feign hypotheses in the absence of knowledge.

 **E.** He counseled the admission of ignorance absent data (this constituted his link to Locke).

 **F.** The following were additional Newtonian goals.

  **1.** Newton's system underscored God's omnipotence and freedom, in contrast to the "necessary" acts of God deduced by Cartesian rationalism.

  **2.** Design: Newton believed that his system offered empirical and inductive proofs of God.

  **3.** One can see, through nature, to nature's laws and their author, God.

    **4.** This meant, of course, that nature was lawful and knowable: all knowledge was a piety.

    **5.** The greatest legacy of Newtonianism was a sense of order and clarity.

**III.** Conclusion.

    **A.** The method of Newton's achievement inspired great confidence: observation, induction, mathematization of motion, quantitative rather than qualitative knowledge, predictive value, and experiment.

    **B.** God did not intend us for ignorance. We now had a method by which to use our minds.

    **C.** For many, this model could be extended to the whole of knowledge.

**Essential Reading:**

Isaac Newton, *Newton's Philosophy of Nature*, pp. 1–67, 116–134.

**Supplementary Reading:**

Isaac Newton, *The Mathematical Principles of Natural Philosophy.*

**Questions to Consider:**

1. How is it possible for a work that few readers understand to change the way a culture thinks about the world?

2. Looking at current thinking about cosmology, astronomy, and physics, is it obvious that the Newtonians won all of the arguments that they had with the Cartesians?

# Lecture Ten
# John Locke—The Revolution in Knowledge

**Scope:** Philosophers today may not read John Locke with great attention or enthusiasm, but his influence upon the late 17th and the entire 18th century can scarcely be overestimated, because he changed the way that the culture thought about knowledge. The classic distinction between Locke's "empiricism" and Descartes's "rationalism" is overdrawn, however, because both thinkers display elements of each tendency. Locke's empiricism resides above all in his view of the origin of our ideas and in his sense of the implications of identifying that source. Whereas Descartes held that ideas are innate *and* yield truth about the real qualities of the world, Locke held that they are acquired and that we have knowledge only of our experience of the world. Ideas arise either from sensation (the senses) or reflection (the mind's awareness of its own behaviors), with simple sensations and simple reflections combining to form complex ideas. Our knowledge is thus limited strictly to our experience, and we must humbly admit our ignorance of the real essences of things. Locke appears to lean toward Cartesian mind-body dualism, but he believes the philosophical issue to be unprovable. The problem for Locke is not to know *what* the world is—we are not made for such knowledge—but to know *how* the world behaves.

**Objectives:** Upon completion of this lecture, you should be able to:

1. Explain why Locke is more important to 20th-century intellectual historians than to 20th-century philosophers.

2. Compare Locke and Descartes on the criterion on truth.

3. Summarize Locke's explanation of the origin of ideas (sensation and reflection).

4. Explain Locke's distinction between real and nominal essence.

5. Give an account of why Locke insists that philosophy often must admit ignorance.

# Outline

**I.** Although Locke is not highly thought of by $20^{th}$-century philosophers, his role in intellectual history is almost incalculable in its importance.

    **A.** For one hundred years, Locke was the reigning epistemological authority in Europe, where his thought wielded great influence.

    **B.** One's epistemology (theory of knowledge) sets the foundation and framework of one's thinking about all areas of human thought.

    **C.** Locke provided the epistemological foundations for the scientific achievements of the $17^{th}$ century.

**II.** Rationalism Versus Empiricism—Descartes Versus Locke.

    **A.** The distinction between Descartes's rationalism and Locke's empiricism has been overdrawn. For example, Descartes advances a mechanistic and empirical natural science, and Locke advances a rationalistic criterion of truth.

    **B.** The real debates between them have to do with:
        **1.** The goal of fundamental natural philosophy.
        **2.** The source of our ideas, and what follows from identifying that source.

    **C.** What is the goal of fundamental natural philosophy?
        **1.** According to Descartes, its goal is truth about the real qualities of the world.
        **2.** According to Locke, its goal is knowledge of our experience of the world. We cannot know things in themselves.

    **D.** What is the source of our ideas?
        **1.** According to Descartes, all of our ideas are innate.
        **2.** According to Locke, all of our ideas are acquired through experience.

    **E.** For Locke, if the issue is certain rational truth, the criterion is intuitive certainty. Our knowledge of the world, however, is known only by acquired ideas.

**III.** The Role of Experience.

    **A.** For Locke, all ideas are acquired by two kinds of experience.

1. Sensation—From our sense experience we acquire ideas about the external world.
2. Reflection—The mind is aware of its own experience in operating upon ideas derived from sensation. From reflection, we derive all ideas relating to volition.

B. Simple sensations or reflections combine to form complex ideas, just as molecules are constructed from atoms (reflecting the influence of Pierre Gassendi).

C. There are no innate ideas; thus, our knowledge is limited to our experience of the world and our own minds.

D. We have no knowledge of what underlies experience.
1. We have no rational knowledge of mind and matter.
2. Locke distinguishes between nominal and real essence.

E. For Locke, this admission of ontological incapacity is proper humility.
1. Although Locke leans toward dualism, he denies that we have knowledge of that dualism.
2. We need to admit ignorance.
3. We need to abate and lessen the claims of philosophy.
4. Those who claim that matter is incapable of thought are impiously denying the omnipotence of God.

IV. Conclusion: The Lockean agenda.

A. The problem, then, is not to know what mind is, but how, in experience, mind behaves. The problem is not to know what matter is, but how, in experience, the world behaves.

B. Since such knowledge is based not on logic but on experience, it is always open to correction by further experience.

**Essential Reading:**

John Locke, *An Essay Concerning Human Understanding*, Book II.

**Supplementary Reading:**

John Locke, *An Essay Concerning Human Understanding*, Book I.

**Questions to Consider:**

1. In what ways is Locke more optimistic, and in what ways is he more pessimistic, than Descartes concerning the prospects of human knowledge?

2. In what ways is Locke "Baconian" and in what ways not?

# Lecture Eleven
# The Lockean Moment

**Scope:** Locke's epistemology shapes the thinking of the entire 18<sup>th</sup> century, occasioning and reinforcing a revolution in the culture's sense of the nature (and limits) of knowledge. In Locke's view, the mind begins as a blank slate on which experience prints ideas via the senses and via reflection. Propositions about the world depend upon those acquired ideas, which in turn depend upon their relationship to experience. We cannot know what is not within our experience, and because experience is not logically determined, our knowledge of the world is merely probable.

For early modern readers and thinkers, Locke's model demystifies the world of knowledge and ideas. However complex a proposition or system, if it is based upon reality it can be broken down into its component ideas, all grounded in experience, and those ideas may be tested against the behavior of the world. Although some later authors will attempt to mechanize Locke's model of mind, that model insists that the mind is an active agency.

The implications of Locke are dramatic: we learn our ethical ideas from experience; we are products of our environment, which, if changed, would change the kinds of human beings it produces; our character and senses of world are therefore relative to time, place, circumstance, and experience. Locke does not regard the implications of his system as dangerous for religion, and he undertakes a work of empirical Christian apologetics, *The Reasonableness of Christianity*, to demonstrate that the truth of Christianity follows empirically from the evidence of the historicity of Christ's miracles and from the evidence of the fulfillment of prophecies.

**Objectives:** Upon completion of this lecture, you should be able to:
1. Summarize Locke's notions of *tabula rasa* and active mind.
2. Explain the implications of Locke's system for the testing of claims of knowledge.
3. Describe the implications of Locke's system for our understanding of the development of character, beliefs, and morals.

**4.** Distinguish Locke's ego-psychology from that of Hobbes.

**5.** Explain Locke's "empirical" defense of Christianity.

# Outline

**I.** Locke's epistemology will become the dominant theory of knowledge in the 18<sup>th</sup> century, effecting a vast revolution in the culture's sense of the nature and limits of natural knowing. What were its essential qualities?

   **A.** In Locke's model, the mind is a *tabula rasa*—a blank slate—on which nature imprints ideas via sensations and in which the mind becomes aware of its own operations on sensations, via reflection.

   **B.** Some ideas attract each other (association).

   **C.** Mind is active, and by abstraction and combination it forms complex ideas.

   **D.** From these ideas it forms propositions, but propositions about the world may be only probable, and they depend for their probability upon their relationship to experience.

**II.** Locke's model leads to a demand for analysis, clarity, and confirmation.

   **A.** In theory, any proposition may be analyzed into its component ideas, then into its component sensations and reflections, and it may be judged in relationship to actual experience.

   **B.** The world of real knowledge becomes, by analysis and experimental confirmation, a lucid world, an accessible and unmystifying world, devoid of obscurity.

   **C.** Take what was complex, and analyze it into its simple parts; confirm or disconfirm propositions about the world by comparing them to the behavior of the things described.

   **D.** These become, in many ways, the mission of the 18<sup>th</sup> century.

**III.** The implications of Locke's model.

   **A.** Some in the 18<sup>th</sup> century will try to mechanize Locke's view of the mind and knowledge (e.g., Helvetius, "to sense is to judge"). This view distorts Locke, however, as Rousseau will see clearly.

**B.** For Locke, sensation means merely to acquire an idea. There is no direct route from sensation to human judgment; the mind is an active agency.

**C.** For Locke, we also learn ethical ideas by experience. We call good what causes well-being; we call evil what causes pain. This model, if not joined by Providence, would be subversive.

**D.** According to Locke, Divine Providence governs what causes us well-being or pain. God has so constructed the world that we learn of good and evil through experience.

**E.** This ethical theory has the following implications:
  1. Environmentalism—people's ethical perceptions will hinge on what the environment rewards or punishes.
  2. Relativism—if our ideas are limited by experience, then all are relative to the circumstances of our own lives.
  3. Character *develops*; there is no essential, fixed character.

**F.** Locke bequeaths two problems to the 18th century:
  1. The specter of philosophical Idealism: if we know only our ideas, does anything exist in the external world that corresponds to our ideas?
  2. Locke's epistemology raises a dramatic question: how to base religious belief upon empirical knowledge.

**G.** Locke's own empiricist apologetics was entitled *The Reasonableness of Christianity* (1695).

## Essential Reading:

John Locke, *An Essay Concerning Human Understanding*, Book IV.

## Supplementary Reading:

John Locke, *An Essay Concerning Human Understanding*, Book III.

———, *The Reasonableness of Christianity*.

## Questions to Consider:

1. Why would readers find Locke's epistemology to be the theory of knowledge embodied in Newton and other experimental scientists?

2. For many readers, Locke removed the danger of Hobbes from empirical philosophy and from the belief that ethics were learned by experience of pleasure and pain. Were they correct?

# Lecture Twelve
# Skepticism and Calvinism—Pierre Bayle

**Scope:** Despite his obscurity for most 20th-century readers, the fideist Pierre Bayle was one of the most influential authors of the late 17th and early 18th centuries. The fate of Bayle's reputation in the 18th century reveals the paradox of urging fideism and the incompatibility of reason and faith in an age of growing confidence in reason. Seen in the context of his Huguenot (French Calvinist) setting, first in France and then in the Huguenot refuge in Holland, Bayle's religious itinerary permits us to understand his themes in the terms of his own commitments. For Bayle, as revealed, for example, in his discussions of the ethics of King David and of the problem of evil under an infinitely good God, human reason is simultaneously vital and critical, on the one hand, and, on the other, incapable of understanding the mysteries of the faith, especially those regarding God's ways with mankind (which is precisely why they are mysteries and precisely why there is need for faith). The arrogance of reason and the avoidance of a simple, peaceful faith, Bayle believes, lead to superstition, intolerance, and cruelty. The irony of Bayle's work is that despite his pious intent, he was increasingly read as irreligious because his fideism confronted a learned world that was ever more naturalistic and committed to reason.

**Objectives:** Upon completion of this lecture, you should be able to:

1.  Describe the changes and reversals of Bayle's reputation.
2.  Describe Bayle's relationship to Calvinism and the Huguenot community.
3.  Explain the theological and political problems addressed by Bayle's article on King David, including the problem of justification and sanctification.
4.  Summarize Bayle's arguments for the insolubility of the problem of evil.
5.  Explain the difficulty of maintaining fideism in an age of increasing commitment to the powers of human reason.

# Outline

I. Although he is not widely known today, Pierre Bayle was one of the most influential authors of the $17^{th}$ century. His appeal lasted throughout the first half of the $18^{th}$ century, when he was one of the most widely-read figures of the age.

    **A.** The case of Pierre Bayle is remarkable and illustrative of $17^{th}$-century tensions and dilemmas.

    **B.** Bayle was known in his own time as an extremely erudite and pious Huguenot. Later, he was adopted by the French Enlightenment thinkers as one of their own.

    **C.** The revision of that view began in the mid-$20^{th}$ century.

    **D.** Bayle had extraordinary influence. His *Historical and Critical Dictionary* was the most widely owned book in private libraries in France throughout the $18^{th}$ century.

    **E.** Bayle has a pious but problematic goal: in order to humble reason and to show our absolute dependence upon faith, he seeks to demonstrate the incompatibility of reason and faith.

II. Knowledge of Bayle's career allows us to place his intellectual work in context.

    **A.** Bayle's religious career demonstrates his intimate ties to Huguenot Calvinism.

        **1.** He was born into a Huguenot family but converted from Protestantism to the Catholic faith.

        **2.** After a few years, he reconverted dangerously to the Reformed faith.

        **3.** He spent long years as a Calvinist teacher.

        **4.** He had an ongoing role as a leading Calvinist polemicist while in exile in Rotterdam.

    **B.** Bayle's publishing career reveals his central position in $17^{th}$-century erudition and debate.

        **1.** Catholics saw him as a Calvinist apologist, while among Calvinists he offended the factions to which he did not belong.

        **2.** The *Historical and Critical Dictionary* had extraordinary success.

III. Bayle's intellectual itinerary.

**A.** Critical reason prepares one for faith. Faith must not fear critical reason or erudition.

    **1.** Bayle writes, for example, that King David was favored by God despite his manifest sinfulness.

    **2.** In response to Pierre Jurieu and the Huguenot community in Rotterdam, who advocated a Protestant crusade against Louis XIV, Bayle urged pacifism.

    **3.** King David, as depicted in Bayle's article, was uncomfortably reminiscent of Louis XIV.

**B.** Bayle raised the following religious issues.

    **1.** The mystery of salvation—God's decisions regarding whom to save surpass all human understanding.

    **2.** Justification and sanctification.

**C.** Bayle raised the following intellectual issues.

    **1.** One should rely only on faith, whatever the scandal.

    **2.** For there to be faith, there must be an obligation to natural judgment.

    **3.** The problem of evil (addressed in three articles): neither logic nor evidence can overcome someone who doubts the goodness of God. Natural reason cannot explain why God allows evil.

**D.** Bayle stages a debate between Christianity and Manicheanism. Reason is not sufficient to defeat the Manicheans. Only faith resolves the paradoxes.

    **1.** For Bayle, all areas of human belief show the incapacity of reason and the need for faith; e.g., the Trinity, the problem of motion, Zeno's paradoxes. Bayle's skepticism is directed against all intellectual confidence.

    **2.** The resolution of Bayle's tensions: humility, tolerance, quiet belief by faith and conscience.

**IV.** Conclusion.

**A.** Opposed by outraged theologians, Bayle attempts to criticize the very foundations of his culture's intellectual inheritance, trying to show that Christianity becomes superstitious when it departs from simple faith.

    **1.** Bayle decries fear of comets and witchcraft belief; the denigration of universal consent; he defends the reality of virtuous atheists.

      **2.** Always, for Bayle, one must avoid overextension of human claims and hold to simple faith.

**B.** A tidal change was occurring in the culture, however, that affected perceptions of Bayle.

      **1.** Bayle was increasingly read as irreligious, given the growing commitment to rational and evidential belief.

      **2.** Bayle's "David" gives rise to Voltaire's "David," despite the extraordinary difference in their two religious worlds.

      **3.** Fideism persists in Europe, but it is occurring on a wave of naturalization and rational commitment.

      **4.** A religious culture rapidly is abandoning the belief that the world is clearer if reason's light is diminished.

## Essential Reading:

Pierre Bayle, *Historical and Critical Dictionary* (Richard H. Popkin, editor and translator), pp. 45–63, 144–153, 166–209, 350–388, 396–444.

## Supplementary Reading:

Walter Rex, *Essays on Pierre Bayle and Religious Controversy*.

## Questions to Consider:

1. By the 18<sup>th</sup> century, many readers viewed Pascal's fideism as sincere and Bayle's fideism as insincere. Is there something about Bayle's arguments that encouraged that reading?

2. Why should the traditional argument that the wisdom of the Christian is foolishness to the world cause such scandal in the late 17<sup>th</sup> century?

# Lecture Thirteen
# The Moderns—The Generation of 1680–1715

**Scope:** The generation of readers and authors between 1680 and 1715 was one of the most revolutionary in European history because it was marked by a fundamental change of attitudes toward knowledge and nature. It was not obvious at the time that this change was occurring—scholasticism remained entrenched in the universities, and fideism and mysticism were vital forces in the culture—but the new philosophers were coming to dominate the learned world, winning the debates, interest, and affection of the reading public.

If we examine the attitude of this generation toward the terms of the *disputatio* by means of which we first came to know the scholastics, we see clearly the transformation of European thought in the 17th century. The generation of 1680 to 1715 increasingly rejected the presumptive authority of the past; it increasingly believed induction from data, not deduction from inherited premises, to be the path toward truth; and it made the systematic inquiry into experience, now seen as "the book of nature," the heart of natural philosophy.

Further, the rejection of the presumptive authority of the past in natural philosophy led quite naturally to a rejection of the presumptive authority of the past in general. Europe possessed a growing sense that it had acquired something unique from 17th-century thinkers—proper method—that would alter both knowledge and the human relationship to nature. The new philosophers increasingly created and inhabited new centers of intellectual and cultural change: academies, learned journals, coffee houses, and non-university learned societies. They also popularized and began to extend the arguments of the celebrated figures of the 17th century. Their heroes were Bacon, Descartes, Galileo, Locke, and Newton, from whom they took what was most general, far-reaching, and innovative. They were drawn to empiricism, quantification, and the naturalization of their world view. They increasingly assailed what they took to be superstition, and they brought an end to the persecution of alleged witches. The new philosophers were determined to remove theology from areas not properly within its sphere, and they wished to devise both an independent domain of natural inquiry and a theology consistent with the new knowledge. This raised extraordinary dilemmas concerning miracles, revelation, and ethics, dilemmas that dominated much of 18th-century intellectual life. By the end of the 17th century, we stand at the birth of modern consciousness.

**Objectives:** Upon completion of this lecture, you should be able to:

1. Describe the extraordinary change taking place in the thought and attitudes of the generation of 1680 to 1715.

2. Explain the fate of the criteria of the *disputatio* in the course of the 17th century.

3. Describe the milieux outside the universities that sustained the new philosophy.

4. Summarize the heroes of the new philosophers and what they took from them.

5. Describe the variety of influences of the new philosophy upon religious questions and attitudes.

# Outline

I. The generation of 1685–1715 embodied a fundamental change of attitude toward the means of knowing truth.

  A. This generation overturned the authority of the *disputatio.*
   1. It rejected the presumptive authority of the past and increasingly recognized the rights of natural reason even in the presence of theological authority.
   2. Rather than relying on syllogistic deduction from premises drawn from authority, it relied on induction—the logic of inference from experience.
   3. European thinkers became accustomed to looking to "the book of nature"—i.e., to experiment, experience, and nature.

  B. Thinkers drew an analogy from the 17th-century revolution in natural philosophy to the means of new knowledge and the reexamination of all claims of truth.
   1. There was a growing sense that Europe had acquired something that would alter both knowledge and the human relationship to nature: method.

      **2.** Rightly or wrongly, the awesome accomplishments of 17<sup>th</sup>-century natural philosophy were associated with induction from nature, ordered by reason into laws as general and universal as possible, confirmed by experiment and experience, and, wherever possible, put to the use of mankind.

**II.** The self-image of the "new philosophers" is seen in their emerging heroes. What aspects of 17<sup>th</sup>-century thought provided the foundation for the early 18<sup>th</sup>-century generation of thinkers?

    **A.** From Bacon they took learning from nature and the rejection of the received authority of the past.

        **1.** They learned to reject the Idols of the Theater: automatic deference to received authorities.

        **2.** From Bacon they took induction and the essentiality of method (the metaphor of the path) without reference to theology.

        **3.** They also took the view of knowledge as human power to enhance human well-being and reduce suffering.

    **B.** From Descartes they took the rights of reason.

        **1.** They emphasized the right of philosophy to begin in doubt: believe nothing, absent rational conviction.

        **2.** They also derived from Descartes the quest for order and clarity: the desire to understand the world.

        **3.** They also appropriated Descartes' belief in the human ability to understand the mechanisms by which the natural order is governed.

    **C.** From Galileo they took the freedom of natural philosophy.

        **1.** They looked to nature rather than to human books.

        **2.** Their view of nature was mathematized.

    **D.** From Locke they took his claim that all knowledge arises from and is bounded in experience.

        **1.** They also appropriated his admission of ignorance on matters beyond experience.

        **2.** They adhered to his view that all knowledge is constructed from confirmable units of simple experience, and that all claims of truth may be examined in such a light.

    **E.** From Newton they took the belief that nature was lawful in design and that the human mind could understand these laws.

1. With an understanding of three laws of motion and the law of gravity, both celestial and terrestrial physics fall into place.
2. Nature is lawful and designed: we see through nature to Nature's God.

**F.** It was still very much a mixed intellectual world.
1. Aristotelian scholastics still dominated the universities.
2. Skepticism and fideism were vital, but fideism was formally condemned in Catholic Europe and about to be swept away by the new confidence in natural philosophy.

**G.** The "new philosophers" set the terms of debate and increasingly won the affections of the growing reading public. The public perceived it as having both theoretical strength (Locke) and concrete accomplishments (Newton and the new science).

**H.** This generation identified a new locus of change and influence.
1. Philosophical thought moved beyond the universities and clerical orders, and into the academies, journals, and coffee-houses.
2. A growing secular reading public emerged, with a will to know. People greeted the new philosophers of the 18th century with the same exhilaration with which they read the 17th-century new philosophers.
3. Beyond abstruse philosophy, popularizers of the intellectual revolution were increasingly read.

**III.** The sea-change in attitudes.
**A.** The new philosophy had several distinctive marks, including:
1. Rejection of the presumptive authority of the past
2. Empiricism—all issues are open to inquiry based upon experience.
3. Quantification
4. Naturalization of one's world view, and refusal to attribute physical phenomena to extra-natural causes.

**B.** The new philosophy constituted a cultural and religious revolution.
1. It launched an assault on witchcraft belief, superstition, and enthusiasm.
2. It located God's providence in natural laws.
3. It promoted a new religious aesthetic marked by the rejection of particular (as opposed to general) providence.

**4.** The new philosophy posed problems for belief in miracles as emblematic of particular providence.

**C.** In both England and France at the end of the 17th century and the dawn of the 18th century, we witness an intense scholarly debate between "the ancients versus the moderns."

    **1.** The past may well be superior in its art.

    **2.** But knowledge and science are cumulative.

    **3.** Knowledge creates progress: the more we know about the real causes of things, the more we may change the world according to the heart's desire for human happiness.

**IV.** The new philosophers sought to remove theology from areas not properly its sphere, and to devise a theology consistent with and evolving with advances in natural knowledge.

**V.** By the end of the 17th century, we stand at the birth of modern consciousness: scientific, secular, inquiring, seeking a principle of authority apart from mere tradition and repetition of the past, but tempted by skepticism and leaps of faith, critical, and confused by the range of choices it has created for itself. For better or for worse, we are the heirs of the 17th-century mind, living in its light and in its shadows.

**Essential Reading:**

Alan Charles Kors and Paul Korshin, eds., *Anticipations of the Enlightenment in England, France, and Germany.*

**Supplementary Reading:**

Paul Hazard, *The European Mind, 1680–1715.*

**Questions to Consider:**

**1.** What are the implications of the growing critique of "superstition" and witchcraft persecutions?

**2.** In what ways has the generation of 1680–1715 distorted the intentions of the authors whose works it appropriated?

# Lecture Fourteen
# Introduction to Deism

**Scope:** Deism is a widespread religious phenomenon among the educated classes of Europe in the 18th century. It embodies belief in a God whose existence and goodness are proven by nature, and disbelief in the Judeo-Christian (or any other) tradition and revelation. It also embodies a complete naturalization and generalization of God's providence. God's sole relationship to the creation is through the natural order that reflects His will, which rules out all acts of particular providence—above all, miracles and revelation.

Historians traditionally have distinguished between positive deism (the proof of God and his qualities) and negative deism (the critique of claims of religious revelation and special truth). As critics of Christian culture, deists engage in historical criticism of the veracity and canonicity of Scripture; in moral criticism of the qualities attributed to God by Scripture; and in social criticism of the role of mystery and priesthood in governance. Deists assert rights of freedom of thought, and they refuse to acknowledge any religious truth not established by natural evidence and reason.

One of the best examples of negative deism is the English deist Thomas Woolston on miracles. In an age that demands proof of the historicity of the miracles, Woolston argues for allegorical interpretation of Christ's miracles, given their literal impossibility and contradictions. If they are not literally true, however, the proof of the divine origin of Christianity by reference to the miracles is vitiated.

The deists are marked, above all, by their common contempt for the Christian clergy, whom they see as suppressing reason and free inquiry, separating mankind from its natural birthright, and distorting the natural moral criteria. The struggle between deistic and Christian intellectuals will be one of the defining characteristics of the 18th century.

**Objectives:** Upon completion of this lecture, you should be able to:
1. Describe the distinguishing general characteristics of deism.

2. Explain the religious implications of the naturalization and generalization of providence.

3. Summarize the deistic arguments against seeing the Christian revelation as divine.

4. Describe the anti-clericalism of the deists.

# Outline

I. Deism was the religion and theology of a surprising number of new philosophers in the $18^{th}$ century. It had vast appeal.

    A. There are several simple definitions of deism:

        1. Belief in God, but disbelief in the Judeo-Christian revelation and tradition.

        2. The complete naturalization of Providence.

        3. The complete generalization of Providence (rejection of particular Providence).

    B. From this view, there follows the rejection of revelation, miracles, and any particular relationship to God.

    C. The sufficiency of nature: God has created us in a natural order through which we shall know God and moral law.

II. The roots and dual nature of deism are found in $17^{th}$-century naturalism.

    A. The deists exalted naturalism and offered a critique of authority and tradition.

    B. They were indebted to the fideism of Bayle and to the new critical scholarship.

    C. They were also indebted to Socinianism (anti-trinitarian thought), although the Socinians regarded themselves as Christians.

    D. Traditionally, historians and students of religion have distinguished between two sides of $18^{th}$-century deism.

        1. Positive deism (deistic theology) affirmed the existence and goodness of God, and saw humanity as linked to God through nature.

        2. Negative deism (criticism of orthodox and revealed religion) rejected all claims of revealed religion and critiqued the Judeo-Christian tradition.

**III.** Positive deism.

    **A.** Positive deism posits the existence of a universal God acting through universal providence (laws of nature) and known by universal faculties (sense experience and reason) in a universal medium (nature).

    **B.** How is God known to us? From His work, nature, which is open to our examination by means of the faculties with which He endowed us.

        **1.** Thus God is the Creator and Providential lawgiver through the structure and mechanisms of nature.

        **2.** Those laws are our link to His will (e.g., the pursuit of happiness).

    **C.** God is known to us empirically through design and moral intention.

    **D.** God is also known to us rationally. Tindal argued that God is self-sufficient. What could He, a perfect being, possibly need from the creation? God's goal is the happiness of His creatures.

**IV.** Negative deism.

    **A.** Negative deism offers a critique of revelation.

        **1.** Its historical criticism is applied to the canon, to the veracity of Scripture, to its chronology, and to its sources and science.

        **2.** They also criticize it on moral grounds, decrying the immoral qualities of the Judeo-Christian God, the blasphemy of particularity, and the moral nightmare of Christian history.

        **3.** They observe that mystery in religion promotes the power and privilege of priests, the guardians of the mysteries.

    **B.** Revealed and supernatural religion has separated mankind from its divine natural birthright: senses, reason, pleasure.

**V.** Common deistic themes.

    **A.** True religion must agree with natural reason and evidence; thus true scriptural knowledge is coterminous with knowledge.

    **B.** There is no possible need for revelation, because God has created nature and minds capable of understanding nature and the author of nature.

    **C.** Natural criteria, known to be from God, trump supernatural claims.

**D.** The only individuals who benefit from allegedly mysterious supernatural claims are the self-appointed keepers of the secrets.

**E.** Freedom of thought is always essential, because even the decision to obey authorities is a decision one makes freely. At some level, free thought is a necessity.

    **1.** This freedom of thought alone gives value to one's beliefs and choices.

    **2.** Freedom of thought implies a freedom from arbitrary authority, a human standard of assent, and a human criterion for belief in any creed.

    **3.** Thought alone leads to God. Either we understand God rationally by human, natural criteria, or else we understand nothing of Him and give assent to things we do not comprehend.

    **4.** Claims of particular revelation are always pretense.

**VI.** Deist critique of prophecy and miracles.

  **A.** The English deists argue that in fact the prophecies did not come true.

    **1.** Such claims show a great lack of historical knowledge.

    **2.** They are accomplished only by the most metaphorical and allegorical interpretations of biblical passages.

    **3.** Such a method could prove anything.

    **4.** Examples include Jewish belief in the immortality of the soul; the idea of a chosen people; contradictions in early Church history; and the precariousness of, and the human decisions involved in, the creation of the accepted canon.

  **B.** For deists, the authors of Scripture are very flawed human beings.

    **1.** The authors are accused of anthropomorphism (e.g., portraying God in states of rest, anger, or jealousy).

    **2.** They exhibit pre-scientific superstitions (e.g., talking snakes; Moses and the Pharaoh's magicians).

    **3.** The Jews and Christians projected vile human traits onto the Deity (e.g., Joshua and the slaughter of the innocents).

    **4.** They invest God with vulgar ignorance (e.g., Christ saying that a seed must die before it could bear fruit).

  **C.** The best example of negative deism is Thomas Woolston's discourse on miracles.

1. He argues for "allegorical" interpretations, all based on the impossibility of the supposed miracle and on the greed and fraud of the clergy.
2. Woolston was really saying that the literal miracles did not occur. If that is so, then what of the proof of revelation by scientific evidence of miracle?

VII. Conclusion: The heart of the deist critique of revealed religion and its traditions.
   A. The deists embody a striking hatred of the Christian clergy and their role, and a contempt for the Judeo-Christian portrayal of God in Scripture.
   B. God, for the deists, has revealed Himself to us in nature.
   C. Mankind, from God's loving creation, is self-sufficient.
   D. We have been deprived of this knowledge by those who deny reason, the natural faculties and inclinations, and who deny the natural right and moral criterion, from God, of human happiness in this natural world—in short, by the Christians.

**Essential Reading:**

Matthew Tindal, *Christianity as Old as the Creation.*

**Supplementary Reading:**

Peter Gay, ed., *Deism: An Anthology.*

**Questions to Consider:**

1. In what ways (or not) is deism an application of 17th-century natural philosophy to questions of religion?
2. To what extent is deism a moral rather than historical critique of Christianity?

# Lecture Fifteen
# The Conflict Between Deism and Christianity

**Scope:** In one sense, the conflict between deism and Christianity, which would influence so much of 18$^{th}$-century intellectual life, reflected the recurrent tension, in all cultures informed both by "Athens" and "Jerusalem," between the God posited by philosophy and the God worshipped by the pious. In its most particular sense, however, deism reflected, in its rejection of the God of the Hebrew and Christian Testaments, the first fundamental challenge to Judeo-Christian theology to emerge strongly within Christian culture itself. Deists and Christians clashed over the most essential theological issues: the source of our knowledge of God, the manifestation of God's love and providence, the relationship of God to His creation, the grounds of religious belief, the problem of evil, sin, morality, the goal of life, and the secular implications of religious truth. Although Christian theologians themselves disagreed intensely and creatively on a host of issues, they were united what they shared in opposition to the deists: a belief in a supernatural reality of revelation, particular providence, divine intervention in human history, sin and redemption.

**Objectives:** Upon completion of this lecture, you should be able to:

1. Summarize the main points of conflict between deistic and Christian thinkers.

2. Explain the deistic-Christian debate over particular providence.

3. Describe the deists' confidence in the sufficiency of nature.

4. Explain the importance of the problem of evil to the deistic-Christian debate.

## Outline

I. There is recurrent conflict and tension, independent of deism, between the God of the philosophers and the God of the pious.

**II.** Christians and deists engaged in fundamental debates on a variety of important topics:

    **A.** Knowledge of God

        **1.** The Christian stresses the insufficiency of natural knowledge alone and the need for resort to God as revealed through the supernatural.

        **2.** The deist looks to God as made manifest by nature to the senses and understanding.

    **B.** God's love

        **1.** The Christian holds that God so loved the world that He became incarnate as Jesus, who died to offer redemption.

        **2.** The deist holds that God so loved the world that He created it with the means of redemption always present in nature, always at hand.

    **C.** Creation

        **1.** The Christian views God as the creator of the world in seven days, some 6,000 years ago, and as the creator of Adam and Eve.

        **2.** The deist views God as the creator of the material universe, the Newtonian world order, and the laws of nature. When, how, and in what modes He did so was a matter for science to investigate.

    **D.** The Relation of God to His Creation

        **1.** The Christian emphasizes the particular relations of God with creation, and above all with mankind, and he stresses the efficacy of prayer.

        **2.** The deist emphasizes the universalistic relations of God with creation, and he denies the efficacy of prayer.

    **E.** Revelation

        **1.** The Christian believes that God granted a particular revelation to the Jews; He granted a historically particular but universally available revelation to Christians through Scripture and the operations of the Holy Spirit.

        **2.** According to the deist, God reveals Himself universally through nature and science.

**F.** Belief
    **1.** The Christian identifies a category of religious belief that is acquired through faith, but which is not necessarily contrary to reason and evidence.
    **2.** The deist accepts religious belief that is acquired only through evidence and reason.

**G.** Intervention of God
    **1.** The Christian believes that God intervenes in imperfect nature to achieve His will. He accepts the reality of miracle, prophecy, and gifts of the Spirit, and he views history as providential, reflecting God's loving intervention. Secondary causes constitute the usual course, but God is free to leave them operative or suspend or alter them.
    **2.** The deist denies that God intervenes, since this would contradict the perfection of creation. God's will is immutable. The history of the world is providential only in an ultimate sense. God's will is manifest in the laws of nature.

**H.** The Goal of Life
    **1.** For the Christian, the goal of life is the glory of God and the salvation of the soul; there is a world to come, with one's ultimate destination for eternity in hell or heaven.
    **2.** The deist views the goal of life (from natural revelation) as happiness on earth. There might or might not be an afterlife in which the virtuous are particularly rewarded, but this does not alter the goal of life, and there is no hell, the existence of which would contradict the goodness of God.

**I.** The Problem of Evil
    **1.** The Christian regards physical evil as incomprehensible—who is man to question God?
    **2.** The deist is committed to philosophical optimism and views physical evil as an illusion. All things contribute to the general good.

**J.** Sin and Wickedness
    **1.** The Christian argues that man's fall from grace accounts for human wickedness.
    **2.** The deist denies the existence of original sin, and he sees wickedness as *contra natura*. Man is ignorant, betrayed, deceived, and misled, above all by particularistic religions.

**K.** Morality
   1. The Christian believes that man has fallen beyond the means of self-redemption. He needs grace in order to fulfill his highest possibilities (charity, love, faith). However, there is a growing anti-Calvinism that takes a more positive view of human nature.
   2. The deist views man as self-sufficient, possessing providential natural instincts, and, for most deists, a natural moral sense. Our goal as natural creatures is to fulfill our heart's desire for happiness.

**L.** Secular Needs for Moral Achievement
   1. The Christian emphasizes restraint and religion. After redemption, however, the saved Christian enjoys a Christian freedom.
   2. The deist emphasizes enlightened self-interest; natural instincts are allowed to develop in freedom.

**Essential Reading:**

E. Graham Waring, ed., *Deism and Natural Religion.*

**Supplementary Reading:**

C.J. Betts, *Early Deism in France.*

**Questions to Consider:**

1. What is the most fundamental point of disagreement between deists and Christians?

2. In retrospect, has much of deistic thinking become a part of what now is called "Christianity"?

# Lecture Sixteen
# Montesquieu and the Problem of Relativism

**Scope:** Although the intellectual revolution of the 17th century did much to increase the culture's sense of the commonality and communicability of knowledge about nature, it also raised the problem of relativism. If, as Locke believed, knowledge and moral ideas were caused and bounded by one's experience, then one's sense of the world would be relative to one's time, place, personal experience, and physical senses. This notion of the relativism of knowledge and values was given dramatic impetus by the increasing European interaction with foreign peoples and cultures. That contact provoked not only great curiosity, but a growing awareness of differences among cultures that appeared to extend to fundamental areas of belief, morality, and the ability to communicate.

Montesquieu's *Lettres Persanes* (*Persian Letters*) were a great success in the 1720s, not only because of their exoticism, but because they obsessed upon and explored the problem of the relativism of human perspectives, a problem made more vivid to him by his own personal experiences in the world of learning (experiences that put him in contact with scholars of both distant and ancient worlds). While Montesquieu uses his fictional Persian travelers to satirize and criticize much of Western and, in particular, French life, he also poses the central two questions of his concern: "What is relative to time and place? What is natural and universal?" He links these two domains—the relative and the natural—by exploring the reality of difference and the reality of natural consequences. Human beings may live and believe in a startling variety of ways, but there is a reality principle of objective natural consequences that set limits to our malleability and to our systems. Awareness of relativism, for Montesquieu and for Voltaire, should lessen national and religious arrogance, but it should not blind us that nature, not human wish, determines our common and objective ground. In matters so essential to human life as the relationship between men and woman (the subplot of the harem) or the organization of society (the parable of the Troglodytes), Montesquieu concludes, variety prevails, but there are objective conditions of justice and survival that we ignore at our peril. Despotism is all too real, but it is objectively against nature and inherently unstable.

**Objectives:** Upon completion of this lecture, you should be able to:

1. Explain how the problem of the relativity of knowledge arises from the premises of Lockean empiricism.

2. Describe the importance of travel and missionary literature to European debates of the 18$^{th}$ century.

3. Explain the tension between relativism and naturalism in Montesquieu's thought.

4. Give an account of how Montesquieu uses his account of the cyclical history of the Troglodytes to reveal both the relativism and the objective realities of ethical and political systems.

5. Summarize Montesquieu's view of despotism.

# Outline

I.   18$^{th}$-century relativism had several general sources.

   **A.** Despite its obvious encouragement of seeing knowledge as social and communicable, Lockean epistemology carries within it the seeds of relativism.

      **1.** If one's knowledge and moral ideas are bounded and determined by one's experience, then one's sense of the world, one's values, and one's beliefs are relative to time, place, and personal experience.

      **2.** Locke's doctrine of nominal and real essences establishes that we know only the appearances of things.

      **3.** Locke's doctrine makes one's beliefs relative to the nature of the human senses.

   **B.** Europe's encounter with foreign and "exotic" peoples (the effect of which was multiplied by the growth of printing and the reading public) produced curiosity about and astonishment over differences among cultures, and an awareness that Europeans seemed as strange to others as others did to them.

      **1.** Europeans were struck by the differences between their own and other cultures with regard to the treatment of women and the elderly, and the diversity of religions, moral codes, and beliefs.

    **2.** They were struck by difficulties of translation and by the very fact of flourishing non-Christian cultures.

    **3.** Voltaire began his history of the world with an account of China.

    **4.** Best sellers of the era included *The Turkish Spy*; *1001 Nights*; and accounts of American Indians.

**II.** Montesquieu's relativism has additional sources.

    **A.** His background makes him sensitive to difference and particular perspectives.

        **1.** The milieu of the *parlement* of Bordeaux inculcates an awareness of absolutism and of arbitrary power.

        **2.** His Huguenot (Protestant) wife inculcates an awareness of toleration and of the accident of birth.

    **B.** His intellectual encounters after he comes to Paris dramatically heighten his sense of the relativity of beliefs.

        **1.** He meets with the savants at the Academy of Inscriptions.

        **2.** Montesquieu's educated Chinese friend had converted to Christianity in China. After coming to Europe, he was astonished at the hypocrisy of the supposedly Christian Europeans.

**III.** Montesquieu's *Persian Letters* enjoyed extraordinary literary success.

    **A.** The *Persian Letters* is an epistolary novel in which "Persian" travelers see France and the West through Persian eyes. This device allows Montesquieu great freedom to comment on his world and to deepen his readers' sense of the relativity of belief to time and place.

    **B.** The Substance of the *Persian Letters*

        **1.** The pope, the king, nobles, and bishops are viewed through "Persian" eyes.

        **2.** Montesquieu makes light of ethnocentrism: a Frenchman asks, "How could anyone be a Persian?"

        **3.** Montesquieu asks: "What is relative to time and place? What is natural and absolute?" He seeks to distinguish between what is malleable and what is common to all human experience.

4.  The implications for politics: we see varieties of despotism everywhere, but we also see indications of a natural law of liberty.
5.  The implications for religion: there are varieties of dogma, but we also see a natural law of God's justice and truth.
6.  The implications for ethics: we see various moral codes but also the reality of natural consequences.
7.  The implications for psychology: we see a great variety of male-female relations and of human self-images, but we also see evidence of the permanence of human nature.
8.  The implications for philosophy: we see various approaches to knowledge but also the singularity of natural truth.

IV. Montesquieu in the *Persian Letters* and Voltaire in his "philosophical tales" increasingly speak for the consensus emerging in the French Enlightenment.

A.  Science is a unifying truth amid the relativities of perspective.

B.  Our common ground is set by nature's reality principle, not by human wish.

C.  For both Montesquieu and Voltaire, an awareness of relativism should lessen national and religious pride.

D.  For both, that awareness should promote tolerance and move us toward what we have in common as human beings: empirical science, the recognition of natural needs and consequences, and worship of the author of nature.

V.  The two most striking tales of the *Persian Letters*—the parable of the Troglodytes and the human reality of the harem—lead to and dramatically illustrate the conclusion that forms of association and government arise in response to specific circumstances, making them relative, but they have real consequences, which are universal.

A.  The parable of the Troglodytes teaches that the realities of survival and death set natural limits to human variation.
1.  The original Troglodytes, naturally wild, need a tyrant in order to survive.
2.  Tyrannized, the Troglodytes rebel anarchically and selfishly. In vicious anarchy, however, they virtually perish.

3. The virtuous Troglodytes succeed and prosper, but they create a luxury which undermines the practice of virtue: they wish to be governed so that they might attend only to wealth.
4. Thus an independent natural reality exists in which behaviors have real consequences, and which points to universal values. Human societies can achieve any number of forms, but they cannot survive unless they solve the problem of linking the individual to the broader society.

**B.** The harem shows both the extraordinary variation in forms of male-female association—which people take to be given wholly by nature—and the enduring problem of despotism in human life.
1. The tale illustrates the contrast between the "freedom" of French women and the enslavement of women to a master's will in the Persian harem.
2. All cultures assume that their particular forms of association are "natural."
3. When the despot is unable to exercise terror, the harem revolts and the laws of nature reassert themselves against the despot's arbitrary will. Only terror makes despotism seems stable and permanent.
4. The irony of despotism: the Persian Uzbek sees all despotism around him except his own.

## Essential Reading:

Montesquieu, *The Persian Letters*.

## Supplementary Reading:

Voltaire, *Micromegas*.

## Questions to Consider:

1. Why don't Montesquieu's relativistic insights lead to a thorough skepticism about all human knowledge?
2. In what ways do European encounters with foreign cultures reinforce tendencies of the 17<sup>th</sup> century's intellectual revolution?

# Lecture Seventeen
# Voltaire—Bringing England to France

**Scope**: Few works had greater impact in popularizing the intellectual revolution of the 17th century and in inaugurating debates that would shape the 18th century in France than Voltaire's *Lettres Philosophiques* (*Philosophical Letters*) from England, published in 1734. Voltaire celebrates English religious, political, commercial, and intellectual liberty, and he popularizes the systems of Locke and Newton. He begins with discussions of heterodoxy, orthodoxy, and toleration in English religious life, linking toleration to the commercial values and prosperity of England, and rebuking by implication an officially intolerant, anti-commercial, aristocratic, and despotic France. While idealizing English life (although not English history), Voltaire celebrates a limited government of laws, legal equality, religious pluralism, philosophical and scientific freedom, and a secular society. He also celebrates English empiricism and new philosophy, which, by the example of inoculation against smallpox (accepted in England but illegal in France), he presents as extraordinarily useful to human life.

To those who argue that the new philosophy is dangerous to society and state, Voltaire replies that it has been the theologians who have fomented civil war and mutual hatreds while the philosophers peaceably communicate with each other and work for the improvement of the human condition. In the *Lettres Philosophiques*, we see the 18th century's expansion of the meaning of "philosophy" and the scope of translating the conceptual revolution of the 17th century for a more popular audience.

**Objectives:** Upon completion of this lecture, you should be able to:
1. Explain the historical significance of Voltaire's *Philosophical Letters* in the dissemination of ideas in the 18th century.
2. Summarize the usefulness of English religious variety to Voltaire's lesson for France.

3. Give an account of what Voltaire most admires (and wants France to learn from) in English political and social life.

4. Distinguish between what is meant by "a government of laws" and by "a government of men."

5. Summarize what Voltaire most admires about English empiricism and natural philosophy.

## Outline

I. The background of Voltaire's *Philosophical Letters* from England.

   **A.** Voltaire's formation had made him a deist, new philosopher, and freethinker prior to his trip to England.

   **B.** Voltaire went to England to avoid the Bastille and punishment for having offended a princely aristocrat.

II. Voltaire's *English Letters* (also called the *Philosophical Letters*) are a celebration of English thought and political life and an assault upon orthodox, absolute, and aristocratic France.

   **A.** Many historians have seen them as the first essential work of the French Enlightenment.

   **B.** In France, their publication produces exceptionally strong condemnation of Voltaire and his lifetime banishment from Paris.

   **C.** Voltaire adopts a narrative voice that moves from native orthodoxy to cosmopolitan heterodoxy, and he uses irony and laughter, allowing the reader to draw his or her own "enlightened conclusions" in response.

III. Voltaire's first six Letters concern the subject of English churches and sects. They introduce his readers to criticisms of the Catholic Church and to a free-thinking discussion of religion.

   **A.** The first four Letters are devoted to the Quakers, whom Voltaire compares favorably not only to the Catholics, but to all established Christian churches.

      **1.** Voltaire's Quakers defend their differences from other Christian churches by appeal to Scripture: the Bible can be used to defend mutually exclusive positions.

      **2.** He portrays the Quakers as shocked by the ceremonialism of other religions.

3. He praises their simplicity, their ethics, their sense of the equality of human beings, and especially their tolerance.

4. Voltaire also criticizes those aspects of their faith shared by revealed and supernatural religion in general. However, he is far gentler than in his usual tone on particular creeds.

5. Voltaire offers a purely secular and sociological analysis of why young Quakers are turning to the Anglican Church. In doing so, he treats religion as a phenomenon that can be studied in wholly natural terms.

**B.** To the extent that the Church of England resembles the French Catholic Church, it is satirized and criticized. To the extent that it deviates from the Catholic Church, it is gently, if ironically, praised.

1. Voltaire criticizes the hierarchical episcopacy.

2. He analyzes the intolerance of churchmen and laments their role in fomenting or aggravating England's wars and civil strife.

3. He praises the clear legal pre-eminence of the state over the Church, and the relatively better morals of the English churchmen.

**C.** Voltaire emphasizes the Puritanism, bitter zeal, and intolerance of the Presbyterians, and he reminds readers of their role in the English Civil War.

**D.** Voltaire praises the intellectual merit and temperament of the anti-Trinitarian Socinians (i.e., the Unitarians), who, of all Christians, are the closest to the deists.

**IV.** Voltaire uses England as a foil to criticize what he sees as the despotism and unenlightened government of France.

**A.** Voltaire idealizes English life. He identifies the following factors as sources of England's success.

1. It has a government of laws, not of arbitrary individual wills.

2. Government power is limited by civil liberties and legal equality.

3. Civil strife, fanaticism, and persecution are limited by means of religious tolerance.

4. Commercial freedom produces a commercial prosperity that allows the individual to serve his own interest in a way that enriches the society at large.

**5.** In English society, the arts and sciences are free, respected, and flourishing.

**6.** For Voltaire, all of these positive qualities are interrelated, each reinforcing the other.

**B.** France—intolerant, anti-commercial, aristocratic and despotic— looks especially unappealing when contrasted with Voltaire's idealized picture of England—tolerant, secular, governed by law and liberty, and engaged in productive commerce.

**V.** Voltaire introduces his readers to (and popularizes) English empiricism, and especially the thought of Bacon, Locke, and Newton.

**A.** In his letter on inoculation against smallpox, Voltaire expresses the philosophy of the Enlightenment in outline: reason and experience allow us to employ a method which saves lives and reduces suffering.

**1.** Knowledge moves us from helplessness to natural understanding to increased happiness.

**2.** All things should be judged by their effects upon human well-being.

**B.** Voltaire urges the French to recognize the superiority of Locke to Descartes.

**1.** He asserts the superiority of empiricism over rationalism as a means of acquiring knowledge of the world from the world. He argues on behalf of Locke's sensationalism and against Descartes's notion of innate ideas.

**2.** Voltaire presents Locke as a man who studies how the mind actually behaves instead of vainly theorizing about the substance or nature of the mind.

**3.** Voltaire defends Locke's argument that philosophical skepticism is the only honest conclusion, since it would be impious to assume that an omnipotent God could not have created matter capable of thought. This is not materialism, but an appropriate recognition of the limits of human knowledge.

**4.** Avoiding metaphysical hypotheses and irresolvable arguments, let us study ourselves and the world through our limited natural faculties.

**5.** Voltaire criticizes theologians who claim that Locke and other philosophers threaten morality and society. He holds that the theologians themselves have bred discord and war.

6.   Voltaire lauds Newton's application of Lockean empiricism to the study of nature.

**Essential Reading:**

Voltaire, *The Philosophical Letters*.

**Supplementary Reading:**

Ira O. Wade, *The Intellectual Development of Voltaire* (read selectively, by interest).

**Questions to Consider:**

1.   Voltaire calls his letters "philosophical." What does "philosophical" mean in that context?

2.   Although Voltaire offers descriptions of England, his agenda is clearly, at some level, moral. What are the values embedded in or implied by his account of English life?

# Lecture Eighteen
# Bishop Joseph Butler and God's Providence

**Scope:** The increasing naturalization of God's providence—locating God's wisdom, love, power, and intentions in the regular order of nature—was not simply a deistic phenomenon, but a tidal current of early modern culture on which both deism and Christian theology were carried. 17th-century inquiry had revealed ordered laws of nature with God as lawgiver, and thinkers increasingly saw those laws as the will of God. Following nature meant following the will of God. In moral theology, this meant the revaluation of the mechanism whereby human beings seek pleasure and flee pain. For naturalizing Christian moral theologians, that "pursuit of happiness" was obviously intended by God and, therefore, was obviously linked to virtue. "Following nature" could mean many things conceptually to early modern thinkers, but to many concerned with locating the will of God in nature, it meant following the purposes for which we had been created, as determined by our constitution and highest qualities.

Thus the revered and pious Bishop Joseph Butler, preeminent moral theologian of the Church of England, argued that human beings were made for happiness and virtue, that our nature conduced to both simultaneously, and that by pursuing happiness by means of our highest qualities—reflection and conscience—we satisfied the essentially identical imperatives of our self-interest and our duty. Butler retained a certain Christian dimension to his moral theories, but they were not essential to those theories, which were wholly discernible from nature. Deists who removed that Christian dimension did not depart from Butler's model. Thus the deist Jefferson's claim that it was "self-evident" that we were endowed by God with the right to pursue happiness did not challenge prevailing Christian doctrine.

**Objectives:** Upon completion of this lecture, you should be able to:

1. Explain the link between the scientific revolution of the 17th century and the emergence of the pursuit of happiness as a natural right.

2. Distinguish among various 18th-century uses of the term "nature."

**3.** Describe Bishop Butler's view of human nature and of human unhappiness.

**4.** Explain why, for Bishop Butler, duty and self-interest coincide.

**5.** Explain why deistic and Christian moral theologies can be so surprisingly similar in the 18$^{th}$ century.

## Outline

**I.** Increasingly, 17$^{th}$-century thinkers saw the ordered laws of nature as the instruments of God's will, wisdom, and purpose.

   **A.** The discoveries of 17$^{th}$-century natural philosophy (science) produced a sense of touching the order and providence of God.

   **B.** The new philosophers saw themselves as profoundly pious minds who had chosen to learn God's designs and purposeful intelligence from what God actually had created.

   **C.** The new science produced a sense of religious awe in locating God's providence in natural mechanisms themselves. Following the empirically discernible laws of nature meant following the laws of God.

**II.** This perception validated physical and secular pleasure as the happiness we had the right, from God, to seek.

   **A.** Christian theology distinguished between *beatitudo* (beatitude—blessed reunion with God in life everlasting) and *felicitas* (earthly happiness).

      **1.** Christian moral theologians long taught that the latter was a fallen, corrupted remnant of the highest calling to pursue beatitude.

      **2.** In the 18$^{th}$ century, that view of *felicitas* changed.

   **B.** The governance of mankind by the pursuit of natural, secular pleasure and the flight from natural, secular pain was, if a primary goal, the mark of our sin and of our distance from God. To the extent that it governed our lives, it indicated that we had not raised ourselves or been raised by God to a higher level of being.

   **C.** In light of the new philosophy of the 17$^{th}$ century, earthly happiness acquired validation.

      **1.** If the laws and mechanisms of nature were the agencies of divine intention, and if it were a law of nature and a governing mechanism that human beings and all other living creatures sought earthly pleasure and fled earthly pain, then it followed that the pursuit of such pleasure was the divinely ordained end of human life.

    **2.** The pursuit of happiness was what God himself had chosen for us and had joined to the good.

**III.** The distinctions among the various meanings of the "nature" created providentially by God allow us to understand the pious meaning of "following nature."

    **A.** The first meaning of "nature" refers to anything empirically observed; it has no moral content. In such a model, all things and phenomena that are not supernatural are natural.

    **B.** The second meaning of "nature" refers to nature as the statistical norm.

        **1.** Understood this way, nature might or might not have moral content.

        **2.** From such a model, it is natural for parents to care for their children; it is unnatural (even if empirically observed) for parents not to care.

    **C.** Finally, we can understand nature as essence (that which distinguishes the creature from all other things). From this model, it is natural for a human being to use reason—his or her distinguishing trait—in interacting with the world.

**IV.** Bishop Joseph Butler used the essentialistic model of human "nature," in his *Fifteen Sermons on Humane Nature*, to argue that before and independent of Christian revelation, our natural knowledge and the ordinary tendencies of our human nature lead us to virtue.

    **A.** We must examine and analyze our purposeful design in order to know our nature.

    **B.** Our essence is to pursuit happiness, governed naturally by reason and conscience.

    **C.** Given the reality of divine design, we know that the pursuit of secular happiness, to which our nature impels us, leads us—when we are governed by reason and conscience—to the good.

        **1.** Against Calvin and Hobbes, he argues that self-love is good and that benevolence and self-love are not in conflict.

2. We must love ourselves if we are to love our neighbors as ourselves. To say that we should not seek our happiness in this secular, natural world was to criticize the very design of God.
   3. There is no inconsistency whatsoever between moral duty and self-love or self-interest. If it is a law of nature that we were creatures of self-love in pursuit of happiness, then happiness is our literal, God-given birthright and coincident with virtue.
   4. For Butler, there remained a minimal Christian dimension to this purely natural moral theology.
      a. For the Christian, the achievement of happiness through enlightened and virtuous self-interest was reinforced by eternal reward and by the particular command of Christ.
      b. Further, the world was not perfect, and the afterlife could make amends for the failure of virtue to secure earthly happiness.
   5. Butler concludes that duty and interest coincide, almost always in this world, but absolutely if we take into account the whole.

V. Thus deism and new philosophical Christianity moved on the same tidal current of conceptual change. Deism did not alter new philosophical Christianity but simply naturalized categorically the religious component of the pursuit of happiness.

   A. The deist Matthew Tindal made the universal laws of nature—including the human pursuit of natural pleasure and avoidance of natural pain—the sole moral connection between mankind and God.

   B. For Tindal, God not only wanted our happiness, He had defined that happiness, through our nature, in terms of the secular pursuit of knowledge, bodily health, and physical pleasures, none of which could offend God.

   C. It was but a small step from Bishop Butler to the deism of Thomas Jefferson, who indeed could assert that it was self-evident that all human beings were endowed by their Creator with the unalienable right to the pursuit of happiness. In making this assertion, however, Jefferson was not challenging 18th-century Christian natural theology, but reaffirming it.

**Essential Reading:**

Joseph Butler, *Five Sermons on Human Nature*.

**Supplementary Reading:**

Knud Haakonssen, *Natural Law and Moral Philosophy from Grotius to the Scottish Enlightenment.*

**Questions to Consider:**

1. Is Butler's Christian moral philosophy compatible with the Christian notions of sin and original sin?

2. For what theological reasons does Butler wish to preserve a positive view of human nature against Hobbes and Calvin?

# Lecture Nineteen
# The Skeptical Challenge to Optimism—David Hume

**Scope**: The first half of the 18$^{th}$ century was the high-water mark of confident and optimistic natural philosophy and natural religion. This confidence was built upon the belief that the natural faculties linked our minds to manifest natural truth, and this optimism was built upon the belief that this truth included knowledge of the beneficent and providential designs of God for us. There were diverse challenges to such philosophical optimism—among them, evangelical religious revival and a critical empiricism—but one of the most dramatic and through criticisms came from the Scottish philosopher and philosophical skeptic David Hume, in his posthumously published *Dialogues Concerning Natural Religion*.

Although the dialogic form in theory commits Hume to no particular position, he gives extraordinary voice to the skeptical Philo, who challenges the fundamental premise of natural religion—that we must infer logically from the data of nature a wise, intelligent, good, omnipotent, and providential God. Philo challenges the very assumption that we can infer the necessary cause of the universe, the analogy between nature and the works of human intelligence, and the inconsistencies between the qualities attributed to God and what we would infer from the operations of nature about the cause of the world. In particular, he argues that the evidence of evil, pain, and suffering does not support such an inference. From Philo's arguments, one might choose to believe in God, but it would not be the product of natural inference in a manner consistent with the new sciences.

With Hume, we see a growing skepticism about the relationship of natural philosophy and religious belief, a skepticism that explains in part the increasing turning away by intellectuals from problems of theology to problems of secular society.

**Objectives:** Upon completion of this lecture, you should be able to:

1. Describe the basic premises of optimistic natural philosophy and natural religion.

2. Summarize Hume's general arguments against the philosophical method of natural religion.

3. Explain why Hume believes we may not infer the attributes of God from the operations of nature.

4. Summarize Hume's treatment of the problem of evil.

## Outline

**I.** 18th-century optimistic natural philosophy and natural theology were founded on two confident conclusions inherited from the intellectual revolution of the 17th century.

    **A.** The first was the belief that the natural faculties, through the medium of nature, linked human beings to natural truth and to knowledge of God.

    **B.** The second was the belief that nature and man interact to the benefit of man, through the providential designs of God.

**II.** Natural optimism faced several other challenges.

    **A.** The proponents of evangelical religious revival denounced as folly the counsel that human beings should follow the inclinations of their nature. In the evangelical view, this naturalism ignored the reality of depravity, the sin and danger of this-worldliness, and man's absolute dependence upon God.

    **B.** Inherent in Locke's empiricism was the skeptical view that knowledge is limited, relative to experience, and, at its best, merely probable.

    **C.** Further, Bishop George Berkeley asked how we know that any external world causes, corresponds to, or is represented by our ideas and images, when all we know are our ideas and images?

**III.** One of the most dramatic challenges to optimistic natural philosophy and natural theology came from David Hume, in his *Dialogues Concerning Natural Religion*.

    **A.** This work challenges the fundamental premise of natural religion: that by inference from the phenomena of nature, we are obliged to infer a cause analogous to a human mind from the order and benevolence of nature, and that this cause is an intelligent, wise, omnipotent, and good God.

**B.** Philo points out in the *Dialogues* that any effort to base religion upon inference from experience has four fatal general flaws.

  **1.** It leaves religion merely probable at best, since knowledge from experience is not logically necessary but determined by ongoing experience.

  **2.** It proceeds on the basis of an extremely weak analogy, since the dissimilarities between the universe and the works of men are far more striking than any similarities

  **3.** The analogy is vitiated by the fact that the universe is the only one of its kind that we know, and we know it very partially indeed. How scientifically can one draw inferences about its necessary or even probable cause?

  **4.** To cite the order of the universe is insufficient, since there is also evidence of disorder, and both require explanation by the cause one assigns. What convinces us that this universe could not have arranged itself by chance?

**C.** Even if one granted the terms of the analogy, we would not logically infer from the universe the God of natural religion. By analogizing from the world, we would infer a cause that does not have the qualities of God.

  **1.** God must have no infinity, since the universe has only finite effects.

  **2.** God must have no perfection, since the world has so many flaws.

  **3.** God must have no unity, because of the diversity of effects in the world.

  **4.** God must have no incorporeality, since we only know work to be performed by material agencies, by hands, by bodies.

  **5.** God must have no intelligence, since the world is not a "machine" requiring an intelligent designer. In fact, the world resembles a vegetable, with growth and decay, more than it does a watch or knitting loom.

  **6.** God must have no supreme wisdom, since human beings improve on the design of nature, and since change is constant even in nature.

**D.** If nature proves the infinite goodness of its cause, then how can we explain the miseries, pains and uncertainties of life? If a parent could save his children from disease, earthquake, plague but chose not to, would we call that parent good and wise?

1.  Finite, imperfect human beings could improve upon nature if consulted.
2.  There are only four logical possibilities to be weighed in light of the evidence. The world as we observe it is explicable only if its cause is (as the natural religionists claim) infinitely good, or if it is infinitely evil, or if it is composed of warring opposites of good and evil, or if it is neither good nor evil. The only tenable explanation is that the cause of the universe is indifferent to good or evil.

E.  In short, although one might choose to believe in God, that belief would not arise from the optimistic perspective that our natural faculties, through the medium of nature, know God and God's goodness and should use nature as their moral guide.

**Essential Reading:**

David Hume, *Dialogues Concerning Natural Religion.*

**Supplementary Reading:**

David Hume, *A Natural History of Religion,* in *Writings on Religion.*

**Questions to Consider:**

1.  We know that David Hume claims atheism to be an absurdly dogmatic position. What distinguishes Hume's rejection of natural religion from atheism?
2.  Is the marriage of philosophy and religion more dangerous to the former or to the latter?

# Lecture Twenty
# The Assault upon Philosophical Optimism—Voltaire

**Scope:** Another pillar of the philosophical optimism discussed in the previous lecture was the rationalist argument afforded to it by the great philosopher Leibniz, whose *Essais de Theodicee* (Essays on Theodicy) of 1710 sought to prove that God would only have created "the best of all possible worlds," and thus that all things in the world serve an ultimate good. This philosophical optimism, as paraphrased by Alexander Pope, insisted that "Whatever is, is right." Linked to the theological empiricism that inferred an infinitely good God from the design of nature, rationalist philosophical optimism reinforced the confidence of natural religion.

By mid-century, there were many reconsiderations of such naturalist optimism, including a rethinking of the issues by Bishop Butler himself. The most influential of these reconsiderations, however, came from the heart of deism itself—from the pen of Voltaire. Obsessing on the problem of evil in the wake of personal and European catastrophes, including the destruction of Lisbon by earthquake, Voltaire wrote a "Poem on the Lisbon Earthquake" that announced the incomprehensibility of evil.

Attacked by Rousseau and others for this work, he replied, after much intellectual paralysis, with his most enduring work, *Candide, or Optimism.* Though often amusing and replete with satire, *Candide* is a dark and serious book that seeks to refute Leibnizian philosophical optimism. According to Voltaire, humanity has needs unmet by theology; philosophical optimism is both fatalistic and inhumane; metaphysics cannot resolve the problem of evil; the world is filled with unredeemed suffering; and the only ease from anguish is to "cultivate" the human garden. *Candide* both reflects and deeply influences the intellectual community's transition from abstract philosophy to a focus on the human condition.

**Objectives:** Upon completion of this lecture, you should be able to:

1. Summarize the arguments of Leibniz's theodicy.

**2.** Explain why the Lisbon earthquake posed such particular philosophical problems to the 18th century.

**3.** Describe Voltaire's reconsideration of the problem of evil.

**4.** Explain how *Candide* attempts to refute a complex philosophical system by means of fiction.

**5.** Distinguish between a skeptical deism, on the one hand, and atheism, on the other.

# Outline

**I.** Despite Hume's challenge to the widespread confidence that the data and evidence of nature required one logically to infer a benevolent God as its author, there were also two powerful currents of purely rationalistic analysis of God that reinforced or enhanced optimistic natural philosophy.

  **A.** Tindal noted that because God is perfect, He lacks nothing and created the world for our happiness.

  **B.** Leibniz's rationalist theodicy had vast and growing appeal until the mid-18th century. God, being omnipotent, omniscient, and infinitely good, necessarily created "the best of all possible worlds."

**II.** Bishop Butler also reconsidered the optimistic conclusions of natural theology.

  **A.** In *The Analogy of Religion, Natural and Revealed, to the Constitution and Course of Nature* (published ten years after his optimistic sermons on the providential design of nature), Butler accounted for the affinity between God's revelation in nature and His supernatural revelation in Scripture by noting that both involved explicability and required a faith that surpassed reason.

  **B.** Both nature and scripture give us enough light and explanation to see the hand of God, but both are mysterious enough that we need faith in order to know God affectively.

  **C.** As the problem of evil shows, the providence of God is not clear in nature. Faith alone reconciles us to providence.

**III.** No apostasy from philosophical and theological optimism was more dramatic or influential, however, than that of Voltaire.

**A.** Voltaire despaired over his personal life, the state of European affairs, and his place within his civilization.

**B.** The destructive Lisbon earthquake of November 1, 1755, seared his consciousness and deeply affected Europe's intellectual life.

    **1.** How can the evil produced by nature's general laws be reconciled with the providence of God?

    **2.** In his "Poem on the Lisbon Earthquake," Voltaire argued that evil is real and incomprehensible. Rather than attempt to understand God, we should devote our love and attention to suffering humanity.

    **3.** Rousseau responded that Voltaire has "betrayed God's providence" by doubting that this is the best of all possible worlds.

**IV.** Voltaire's *Candide*—his most enduring work—constituted his answer to Rousseau and to himself. In it, he attempted to refute Leibnizian philosophical optimism by juxtaposing it, in fiction, against the human condition.

**A.** Candide is the student of Pangloss, whose Leibnizian philosophy appears futile, irrelevant, and absurd in the midst of human pain and suffering.

**B.** Philosophical optimism equals fatalism; if "whatever is, is right," then one's attempts to mitigate suffering do not matter.

**C.** Candide voyages through a world of disease, war, cruelty, natural catastrophe, and endless unredeemed human suffering.

**D.** Candide's conclusion is: "Let us cultivate our garden." The only antidote to pain and despair is to work in the earthly garden, to stave off what suffering and vice we can.

**E.** God's existence is proven by the design of the world, but we do not know that He cares for us.

**F.** This conclusion marks a momentous shift from theological or metaphysical concerns to the human condition.

**V.** The crisis of confidence through which optimistic natural philosophy and theology passed in the mid-18th century transformed the culture and intellectual life of Western Europe in lasting ways.

**A.** Philosophy was displaced.

**B.** It became legitimate to refute formal thought by appeal to human experience.

**C.** Theology was displaced from the center of intellectual activism.

**Essential Reading:**

Voltaire, *Candide.*

**Supplementary Reading:**

Gottfried Wilhelm Leibniz, *Theodicy.*

Voltaire, "Poem on the Lisbon Earthquake."

**Questions to Consider:**

1. Are Hume's philosophical and Voltaire's humanistic critiques of optimism complementary or opposed?

2. By the mid-18th century, philosophy and theology are absorbing less and less of reading public's interest. Given the public's love of the philosophical revolution of the 17th century and its close relationship to theology, how might one explain this fact?

# Lecture Twenty-One
## The Philosophes—The Triumph of the French Enlightenment

**Scope:** The *philosophes* of the French Enlightenment—a diverse community of thinkers and writers who regarded themselves as "new philosophers"—took as their mission the critical reexamination of knowledge, authority, and institutions. Linked by a shared rejection of inherited authority, an embrace of the 17th-century conceptual revolution, the ethical principle of utility, and opposition to the Church, the *philosophes* earned an international audience and won the loyalty of the reading public during the 18th century.

A major agency for the dissemination of Enlightenment ideas and attitudes was the vast and commercially successful enterprise of the *Encyclopedie*, published in 28 volumes between 1751 and 1772 under the editorship of Denis Diderot. The *Preliminary Discourse* of the *Encyclopedie*, written by d'Alembert in 1751, called for the wide diffusion and preservation of the ongoing accomplishments of the great rebirth of method and knowledge in the 17th century. The *Encyclopedie* drew hundreds of authors and experts into its struggle for freedom of expression, and it sought to bring readers to the frontiers of knowledge in philosophy, science, history, the arts and letters, and technology. The Enlightenment in France polemicized sharply for the new experimental methods, for the principle of utility, and for religious toleration, winning the war for public opinion against its adversaries and itself ascending to privilege in the Old Regime. Far from being a unity, however, the Enlightenment embodied intense debates over political change, the meanings of "nature," deism and atheism, optimism and pessimism, and elitism and egalitarianism. An endless series of debates is one its profoundest legacies.

**Objectives:** Upon completion of this lecture, you should be able to:

1. Describe the institutions, shared beliefs, and shared values of what is termed "the French Enlightenment."

**2.** Summarize the main issues of social contention between the Church and the *philosophes.*

**3.** Describe the scope and significance of the *Encyclopedie.*

**4.** Explain the importance of the issue of toleration to the struggle between Church and Enlightenment.

**5.** Explain some of the most profound debates and tensions within the Enlightenment.

## Outline

**I.** In mid-18$^{th}$-century France, a community of thinkers and writers emerged around certain shared attitudes toward the new philosophy, arbitrary authority, and the Church.

    **A.** This community saw itself as part of a meritocratic "Republic of Letters."

    **B.** This generation thought of itself as leading humanity into a new relationship with nature and with natural human society. Empirically derived knowledge would be applied toward the reduction of human suffering and the increase of human well-being.

    **C.** They redefined the meaning of "philosopher" and appropriated the name "*les philosophes.*"

    **D.** They had diverse social and educational origins, but they shared certain values, interests, and opponents.

    **E.** They coalesced around certain institutions—cafes, salons, patrons, academies—and certain ideas.

        **1.** They rejected inherited authority *per se*.

        **2.** They were committed, in theory at least, to empirical evidence, rational analysis, and the belief that nature was our sole source of knowledge and values.

        **3.** They shared the ethical principle of utility: the view that the happiness of the species is the highest value, and that all things may be judged by their contribution either to happiness or to suffering.

**II.** Enlightenment thinkers entered into fundamental conflict with the Roman Catholic Church in France. Most were deists and held that God spoke to mankind through nature alone, and that the priests had usurped and falsified God's voice in sectarian religions.

   **A.** Their argument with the Church centered on the critical issue of tolerance and censorship.

   **B.** It centered on differing histories and analyses of their societies.

   **C.** They debated over the status of traditional authority and supernatural claims.

   **D.** They argued over the priority of secular over religious concerns.

   **E.** Both the *philosophes* and the churchmen regarded each other as their deepest foe.

**III.** One of the major agencies of the organization and dissemination of the Enlightenment was the project of the *Encyclopedie.*

   **A.** The *Encyclopedie* had its origins in a decision in 1746 to publish a French encyclopedia to compete with British publications. The publisher selected a group of scholars to contribute, and he named as editors the Enlightenment thinkers Jean le Rond d'Alembert and Denis Diderot.

   **B.** D'Alembert and Diderot planned a vast work that would be a sanctuary of all acquired knowledge and experience.

      **1.** In conformity with the Baconian and Lockean vision, the Encyclopedia would communicate not simply what we know, but how we came to know it.

      **2.** It reflected the Enlightenment's expanded notion of significant knowledge: not simply philosophy, but also history, arts and letters, and—most interestingly—technology.

   **C.** The Encyclopedia was the great publication of the 18th century.

      **1.** It was a runaway best-seller, frequently sold in pirated editions throughout Europe.

      **2.** It engaged more than 160 writers and some 100 informal consultants, including even some clerical experts.

**IV.** The intellectual vision of the *Encyclopedie.*

   **A.** The tone and agenda were set by d'Alembert's *Preliminary Discourse* of 1751.

      **1.** The 17th century had seen a rebirth of knowledge and a qualitative change in human thought.

**2.** Knowledge was a human power to understand all natural things and to alter what could be altered.

**B.** The Encyclopedia provided a focus and means of diffusion for the new philosophy.

   **1.** It embodied the need to reset the priorities of knowledge; it contained many articles on inventions but none on Jesus Christ.

   **2.** It embodied the need to question the origins and foundations of all authorities, beliefs, and institutions.

   **3.** It embodied the belief—given proper and methodical use of the human mind—in intellectual progress.

   **4.** It celebrated the dynamism of science, technology, and secular inquiry.

**C.** The Encyclopedia, in and of itself, was an education in the need for freedom of inquiry and expression.

   **1.** Frequently attacked and occasionally suppressed, it drew its authors, experts, and readers into the drama of censorship.

   **2.** It found agents of collusion and support in the highest structures of the old regime: the courts, aristocracy, and royal ministries.

   **3.** Its very existence as well as its contents undermined the sacred idols and established intellectual authorities of its culture, and it helped to establish the consciousness of "the party of humanity," or "the party of reason."

**V.** Enlightenment thinkers claimed that much of existing authority is arbitrary, arising from power and tradition alone. They called upon authority in countless domains to justify itself according to the following criteria.

**A.** The first criterion was natural experience.

   **1.** If you change experience, you change the individual.

   **2.** However, the debate over whether the environment or physical constitution has greater impact must be open and empirical, given the commitment to natural experience.

   **3.** Enlightenment thinkers rejected supernaturalism: our knowledge is bounded by natural experience

**B.** The other criterion was utility. Happiness is the ultimate ethical criterion, but it initiates some enduring debates between:

   **1.** Individual happiness versus the happiness of society.

©1998 The Teaching Company.

      **2.**    Physical versus psychological happiness.

      **3.**    The debate over whether there is a happiness to virtue itself.

      **4.**    Chastellux's solution was to judge a society by the amount of time it permits each individual to pursue his or her own private vision of happiness.

**VI.** The *philosophes* produced a voluminous literary output between the 1750s and the 1780s.

    **A.**    The Church was placed on the defensive.

    **B.**    The battle cry and most successful issue of the Enlightenment was toleration, which united the diverse tendencies within Enlightenment thought and which won over first public opinion and then the state itself.

      **1.**    The case of Marmontel's *Belisaire* represented an Enlightenment victory.

      **2.**    Voltaire waged a passionate and ultimately successful campaign against the prosecution, torture, and judicial murders of Calas, Sirven, and La Barre.

    **C.**    The Enlightenment itself rose to privileged status within the *ancien régime*.

    **D.**    The Enlightenment represented a battle for the soul of Europe. Who would advise and teach the culture: the clergy or the secular, naturalist intellectuals?

**VII.** The Enlightenment also embodied profound tensions and debates.

    **A.**    It sought reform, but by whose agencies?

    **B.**    It counseled people to follow nature but disagreed about the meanings of nature.

    **C.**    It was torn between deism and atheism, between optimism and pessimism, and between elitism and egalitarianism.

**Essential Reading:**

Jean le Rond d'Alembert, *Preliminary Discourse to the Encyclopedia.*

**Supplementary Reading:**

Francois-Jean de Chastellux, *On Public Happiness.*

**Questions to Consider:**

1. Is the Enlightenment a continuation of the intellectual revolution of the 17th century or a new phenomenon of its own revolutionary importance?

2. What is the model of the "*philosophe*," of the intellectual, advanced by the Enlightenment?

# Lecture Twenty-Two
# Beccaria and Enlightened Reform

**Scope:** The view that both individuals and societies should seek happiness led the 18$^{th}$ century to place great weight on the role of the legislator, whose task it was to reconcile the general and particular interest. This brought a great interest in the law. One of the most influential works of the 18$^{th}$ century was Cesare Beccaria's *On Crimes and Punishments* (1763), an effort to reform, rationalize, and soften the criminal laws of Europe. The great success of Beccaria's work indicates that he produced a moment of truth in readers who no longer thought in accord with the foundations of many of their institutions. He argued that all legitimate authority among men is secular, derived from the consent of the governed, minimal in its exercise, and justified only by its contribution to human happiness. On the basis of these criteria, Beccaria called for the elimination of theology from the law, the reduction of punishments (including the abolition of torture and the death penalty), clear laws, protection of the accused, rational rules of evidence, and legal equality. His model, and its appeal, indicates the 18$^{th}$ century's increased sense of human possibilities: we seek happiness, we can acquire knowledge about the causes of our happiness or suffering, and we may reform institutions in the light of that desire and knowledge.

**Objectives:** Upon completion of this lecture, you should be able to:

1.  Explain the exceptional importance of the role of the legislator in 18$^{th}$-century thought.

2.  Describe Beccaria's criteria of institutional reform.

3.  Summarize the main features of Beccaria's proposals for reform of the criminal law.

4.  Explain the significance of the role of judicial discretion in Beccaria's thought.

5.  Explain how the major particular reforms urged by Beccaria relate to more general tendencies of 18$^{th}$-century thought.

# Outline

I. From 17th- and 18th-century models of ego-psychology, the need arose to reconcile the particular and general interests.

    **A.** The legislator is charged by law with reconciling these interests. He must find means to prevent certain individuals from interfering with the search for happiness by others.

    **B.** The role of criminal law is to preserve the individual's ability to pursue happiness in his own way.

II. European thinkers in the 18th century examined their institutions and codes and found them incompatible with the new philosophy's analysis of the relationship of humanity and nature.

    **A.** *On Crimes and Punishments* emerged from a north Italian context. Beccaria was part of the Academy of the Fist, whose members met to discuss the works of the French Enlightenment.

    **B.** The intellectual origins of *On Crimes and Punishments* included the acknowledged influence of the French Enlightenment (especially Montesquieu and Helvetius), as well as notions of "enlightened despotism."

III. *On Crimes and Punishments* defined the criteria by which to judge institutions and their reform, and it set out a bold plan of necessary reform.

    **A.** All issues of government must be based on natural judgment and evidence, not tradition.

    **B.** The only just criterion in matters of society is utility, "the greatest happiness of the greatest number."

    **C.** Society must be understood as a social contract in which individuals give up the least necessary portion of their freedom in return for the greater happiness of safety and civil order.

        **1.** This conclusion teaches us the legitimate ends and limits of government: because individuals entered society to secure greater happiness, all authority is justified by that result alone.

        **2.** All law and power must justify itself by demonstrating that it secures the greatest happiness of the greatest number.

    **D.** Beccaria's proposed reforms of belief and behavior show the radical potential of rewriting social theory and practice according to his premises.

1. He seeks to eliminate theology from law, both in defining crimes (categories and severity) and in determining punishment.
2. All punishment must be minimal and purposeful.
3. To allow us to use our natural faculties to pursue happiness, we need a government of laws, not of men. Beccaria argues insistently against judicial discretion.
4. The main function of the judicial system is to protect the accused.
5. Equality before the law must be respected.

IV. Beccaria's model reflects the 18th century's dramatically increased sense of human possibilities with respect to the achievement of happiness, the unprejudicial study of nature, and the use of knowledge to ameliorate human suffering.

V. This worldview changes how we argue for or against things in the medical as well as in the political world, and it raises profound issues regarding the mastery and order that human beings do or do not have over life. The Enlightenment's legacy involves the drive to learn from experience and to reach decisions based above all else on that learning.

**Essential Reading:**

Cesare Beccaria, *On Crimes and Punishments.*

**Supplementary Reading:**

Elie Halevy, *The Growth of Philosophic Radicalism.*

**Questions to Consider:**

1. In what ways is utility a radical and revolutionary moral criterion in the 18th century?
2. What has Western culture accepted and rejected in Beccaria's work?

# Lecture Twenty-Three
# Rousseau's Dissent

**Scope:** Rousseau shared much of Enlightenment thought—above all, its Lockeanism, deism, and commitment to religious tolerance—but his critique of "progress" in the arts and sciences and his celebration of the primitive in original nature constituted a major dissent from prevailing Enlightenment beliefs and a major legacy to future Western thought. For Rousseau, cultural "progress" invariably has led to moral decadence, creating artificial needs and artificial inequalities. Society has made us selfish, vicious, weak, arrogant, and unnatural. We blame God for the ills by which we are surrounded and of which we are the authors, misusing the freedom of the will with which God honored us. Humans formed society by some tragic miscalculation of necessity, and it is a permanent state.

The problem, then, is to recognize the depredations of artificial social life and redeem them to the greatest extent possible. This can be done by returning to the religion of nature (deism), by educating the young by the most natural means available (so that they learn directly from nature itself), and by locating legitimate political sovereignty only in the general will that seeks the good of all over the particular good. The legacy of all of these Rousseauist themes is influential and profound, extending to the counter-culture, movements of "return to nature," Kant's categorical imperative in moral theory, and various benign and not so benign efforts to ground political sovereignty in virtue rather than in numerical majorities.

**Objectives:** Upon completion of this lecture, you should be able to:

1. Describe what links and what separates Rousseau from the French Enlightenment.

2. Explain Rousseau's belief that "progress" and society have removed us from our true nature and made us depraved, artificial beings.

3. Summarize Rousseau's arguments that inequality is artificial, not natural.

4. Explain the connection between Rousseau's deism and his more general philosophy.

5. Describe what Rousseau means by a "natural" education.

6. Explain Rousseau's notion of the "general will."

# Outline

I. Rousseau exploded onto the European intellectual scene with his *Discourse on the Arts and Sciences* (1749), in which he argued from history and reason that progress in the arts and sciences has led us away from virtue, lessening rather than increasing it.

    **A.** According to Rousseau, history shows us that moral decadence always accompanies cultural progress.

        **1.** The simple societies of ancient Egypt, Greece, and Rome were overtaken by profound depravity as they became more cultivated and cultured.

        **2.** The simple Swiss and the American Indians compare favorably to the most cultured Europeans in both virtue and happiness, just as the simple Spartans do to the cultured Athenians.

    **B.** Reason also shows the linkage between cultural progress and moral decadence.

        **1.** The arts and sciences create and then satisfy artificial vices and human pride, serving luxury and vanity, not our natural needs.

        **2.** They lead to laziness and boredom.

    **C.** Rousseau's themes included the celebration of the primitive, the decadence of culture, and the "natural" versus the "artificial."

II. To understand the development of these themes, we first must understand Rousseau's deism and his defense of providence.

    **A.** Rousseau has a passionate and positive deism. He defends the existence and goodness of God against the atheists.

        **1.** He advances a proof of God from motion within a system of inert matter, from the spontaneous motion of living things, and from the ordered and lawful motions of the world.

        **2.** Why do we suffer if God is infinitely good? Rousseau answers that humans, not God, are the source of evil.

      **3.**    He emphasizes God's ongoing love and providence.

  **B.**  Rousseau defends natural religion against the claims and beliefs of revealed religion, especially against the claims of Christianity.

      **1.**    What we know of God, we know from nature and reason, both of which are universal and from God.

      **2.**    Revelation is defended by claims that God required such a means to teach us how to serve Him, but the diversity of cults and revelations belies the efficaciousness of such means.

      **3.**    Christianity confuses the ceremony of religion with the interior adoration of God.

      **4.**    Revealed religion gives God human passions.

      **5.**    Individuals are Christian, Muslim, Jew, or Buddhist merely by the accident of birth and education. Is that how God would reveal Himself to us?

      **6.**    All religions claim extraordinary means to prove themselves (miracles, prophecies, grace). It would take a lifetime of scholarship and knowledge of all dead and living languages to evaluate such claims. Is that how God would reveal Himself?

  **C.**  Rousseau concludes that we should strive to know God through nature and work for that truth. Toleration was the only matter on which he would not compromise.

**III.**  In his *Second Discourse, On the Origins of Inequality* (1755), Rousseau asks whether inequality is natural.

  **A.**  Rousseau's lyrical picture of primitive, pre-social humanity informs us of what we have lost as a result of civilization.

  **B.**  He senses the great tragedy in human history: out of some perceived ephemeral need, we created permanent society.

      **1.**    This society is a dominant, coercively triumphant form of human life that sweeps away the morally superior primitive.

      **2.**    It introduces unnatural forms that create unnatural relationships: property ownership, division of labor, social inequality, and the imposition first of the strong, then of the rich.

      **3.**    Arbitrary power creates and maintains social injustices that we regard as natural, but that are wholly a creation of culture.

      **4.**    The attempt to satisfy artificial needs stifles conscience and natural compassion and breeds selfishness. We are separated from our real (God-given) natures as a species.

       

**IV.** Rousseau proposes two means of partial reparation to our ills: education and setting a new moral foundation to politics.

    **A.** Education—Rousseau's *Emile* seeks to create the greatest amount of natural learning and inoculation against social depravity.

        **1.** The goal is direct education by nature, not by men or things.

        **2.** Education begins in infancy and proceeds by experience, not by rote or books.

        **3.** Form strong bodies and senses, and develop confidence in them.

        **4.** One should develop the intellect by observation and by promoting reasoning in the service of real needs. Let you reinvent the sciences to satisfy basic desires, and let him learn morals from natural consequences and mutually beneficial interactions that depend upon ethical principles and relationships.

        **5.** There should be no religious education until adolescence.

        **6.** You should be taught a useful, honest trade, not a "career."

    **B.** Government—Rousseau argues that a proper understanding of the nature and basis of government can produce moral rather than depraved citizens.

        **1.** Unlike Beccaria's model, Rousseau's social contract insists that all individual freedom is given to the state, such that one's own happiness is one's share of the happiness of the society.

        **2.** When one's self-interest can only be pursued by pursuing the well-being of all others, society becomes a means to overcome selfishness and permit moral beings to exist in civilized society.

        **3.** Only the "general will" has political authority. This has profound democratic implications, since the general will arises from all and applies to all.

        **4.** Legitimacy resides only in the general will, not in an immoral and depraved majority. Thus only the general will is sovereign, not the majority *per se*.

        **5.** Being subject to our moral selves (the general will) forces us to be free and unenslaved to our own or others' artificial power, even while in society.

        **6.** To preserve the general will and the social contract, there must be no factions, no gulf between rich and poor, and no society too large for democratic self-governance.

**V.** The Rousseauist legacy is always present and always active.

    **A.** Civilization brings loss and discontent. We have made ourselves unhappy.

    **B.** There is a species nature which society must seek to restore.

    **C.** Freedom consists in being governed by the general, not the particular, and by virtue, not self- interest.

    **D.** Thus the Jacobins and communal counterculture can lay claims to Rousseau.

### Essential Reading:

Jean-Jacques Rousseau, *Discourse on the Origins of Inequality.*

### Supplementary Reading:

Jean-Jacques Rousseau, *Emile*, Books I and II.

————, *The Social Contract.*

### Questions to Consider:

**1.** In what ways does it make sense to think of Rousseau as a defender or as an opponent of the project of the Enlightenment?

**2.** What aspects of Rousseau's thought have been most appropriated by later thinkers?

# Lecture Twenty-Four
# Materialism and Naturalism—The Boundaries of the Enlightenment

**Scope**: The naturalistic materialism and atheism of the late French Enlightenment reveal the boundaries of 18th-century thought. Despite the culture's increasing naturalism in practice (in science and in explanations of most phenomena), it still believes that motion, life, and human nature all require spiritualist explanations to some degree and that there is a point of naturalist explanation beyond which one runs the risk of atheism.

The work of La Mettrie sought precisely to establish materialism as the only means of scientific or philosophical explanation, to demonstrate that human beings are not a dualism of body and soul but one organic entity, to prove that the transition from animal to human life was gradual and not categorical, and to show that the evidence of the Life Sciences revealed a matter that was alive and vital in specific organized forms, not inert and passive.

Denis Diderot, in his speculative (and often playful) natural philosophy, went further, explicitly arguing on behalf of atheism in science and philosophy. For Diderot, all matter is potentially alive and moves between organic and inorganic states on the basis of natural organization and catalysts, species have transformed on the basis of spontaneous changes and the survival of the best adapted, and human thought and will are the behaviors of the physical body. The ethical implications of this naturalism for Diderot were that the goal of our ethical systems are survival, pleasure, and utility, and that we depend upon truth for our successful interaction with nature. The kaleidoscopic natural world of Diderot marks the ultimate rejection of the purposeful, qualitative world of Aristotelian scholasticism. With atheism, the debates of the modern age begin in all of their intensity.

**Objectives:** Upon completion of this lecture, you should be able to:

1. Describe the ways in which spiritualism persisted strongly in the 18th century.

2. Summarize La Mettrie's arguments for extending materialism to the science of man.

3. Distinguish between La Mettrie's metaphysical skepticism and Diderot's atheism.

4. Describe Diderot's view of the transitions between organic and inorganic entities.

5. Explain Diderot's sense of the ethical implications of materialism.

## Outline

I. Despite increasing naturalization of the 18th-century scientific world view and the marginalization of any practical spiritualism, there remain two areas in which spiritual explanation remains essential.

   A. Naturalistic, mechanistic, and materialistic explanations were increasingly used to understand the physics of bodies and the physiology of living things. Spiritualistic explanations of physical behavior were increasingly seen as an admission of ignorance.

   B. However, metaphysical explanations remained regnant for the origin of acquired motion and the foundation of spontaneous motion.

   C. Above all, however, the spiritualist explanation of human nature and behavior remained influential.
      1. The human soul was viewed as the essential phenomenon of knowing and choice.
      2. There was a general refusal to extend the model of animal behavior to human beings.

   D. The stakes of retaining spiritual explanation was high. Without it, Europe faced the specter of categorical naturalism.

II. La Mettrie and the emergence of explicit materialistic naturalism in the French Enlightenment.

   A. La Mettrie was not admired by later French materialists, since he identified sensual pleasure as the ultimate good.

   B. He had a medical background and deep familiarity with the life sciences. He pursued a total physical medicine that would eliminate spiritual explanations and encompass all aspects of human behavior.

**III.** The following were the primary themes of La Mettrie's *L'Homme Machine* (*Machine Man*, or *The Human Mechanism*).

    **A.** One must make an absolute choice between spiritualism and materialism: there is no middle ground.

        **1.** La Mettrie saw much of Greek philosophy as wholly materialistic.

        **2.** Spiritual explanations are essentially a confession of ignorance and helplessness, an abandonment of inquiry.

        **3.** Materialism is the possibility of human knowledge and mastery. It is an invitation to human exploration of the human phenomenon; a tearing down of boundaries to science.

        **4.** Materialism is a strategy of human knowledge, not a metaphysical truth.

    **B.** The soul or mind is not distinct from the body, but a behavior of the body.

        **1.** Physiology has a tremendous impact on our consciousness and will.

        **2.** Thought and will are correlated to the physiology of the brain and the central nervous system.

    **C.** Human beings are not categorically distinct from other animals; the transition from lower animals to man is gradual and founded upon observable physical differences of constitution.

    **D.** Matter is not inert and lifeless absent an indivisible soul, but alive and vital in specific organizations.

    **E.** La Mettrie concludes that the soul is the effect, not the cause, of the body's behavior. Nature has formed us as organisms capable of thought.

**IV.** Denis Diderot's relationship to Enlightenment atheism.

    **A.** D'Holbach's circle included Diderot and Naigeon.

    **B.** Diderot's atheistic works were published only after his death, although his salons had been preoccupied with his atheist theses.

**V.** Diderot's work displays the following naturalistic themes.

    **A.** The crucial issue is the existence or non-existence of God.

    **B.** All matter (all nature) is potentially alive.

        **1.** There is no categorical distinction between the organic and inorganic.

2. Physical behavior depends upon organization and catalysts.
3. Time and purely natural agencies transform the living into inorganic and the inorganic into the living.
4. Life and death are two modes of the same matter.
5. The hypothesis of God explains nothing, confuses much, and is unnecessary.

C. Diderot offers proto-evolutionary speculations on the transformation of the species over time, the survival of the best adapted, the scientific need to abandon the limitations of Scriptural time, and the cells as carriers of the information of each organism.

D. Human thought is a scientific, not a theological, mystery.

VI. Diderot squarely faces the ethical implications of atheistic naturalism.

A. Ethics as behavior is partly inherited, partly learned.

B. The goal of ethics is survival and better interaction with nature and ourselves.

C. The only ethical criteria are pleasure and utility.

D. For Diderot, atheism is proper humility.

E. Atheism is the ultimate humanism.

VII. Conclusion.

A. Naturalism is the ultimate overthrow of the Aristotelian scholastic system.

B. Naturalism asks to be judged less on philosophical than on historical grounds.

C. In an unplanned universe that does not care for us, there exists the need to coexist with nature and with each other and to build human well-being.

D. The debates of the modern age begin in all of their intensity.

**Essential Reading:**

Denis Diderot, *D'Alembert's Dream.*

Julien Offray de La Mettrie, *Machine Man*, in Ann Thomson, ed., *La Mettrie: Machine Man and Other Writings.*

**Supplementary Reading:**

Alan Charles Kors, "The Atheism of d'Holbach and Naigeon," in Michael Hunter and David Wootton, editors, *Atheism from the Reformation to the Enlightenment*, pp. 273–300.

**Questions to Consider:**

1. Does scientific naturalism in any way demand atheism as its philosophical complement?

2. Is Diderot one logical conclusion of the intellectual revolution of the 17<sup>th</sup> and 18<sup>th</sup> centuries, or is he the beginning of something essentially new?

# Timeline

1543 .................................................Publication of Copernicus's heliocentric theory.

1561 .................................................Birth of Francis Bacon.

1564 .................................................Birth of Galileo.

1571 .................................................Birth of Kepler.

1588 .................................................The defeat of the Spanish Armada; the birth of Thomas Hobbes.

1596 .................................................Birth of Descartes.

1598 .................................................Edict of Nantes in France grants limited toleration to the Huguenots (French Calvinists).

1605 .................................................Publication of Bacon's *Advancement of Learning.*

1609 .................................................Kepler publishes his *Astronomia Nova,* asserting the elliptical orbit of Mars.

1618 .................................................Bacon becomes Lord Chancellor of England; beginning of the Thirty Year War in Europe.

1620 .................................................Publication of Bacon's *Novum Organum.*

1621 .................................................Bacon disgraced for bribery and returns to private life and thought.

1623 .................................................Birth of Pascal.

1626 .................................................Death of Francis Bacon.

1628 .................................................Death of Kepler.

1632 .................................................Birth of Locke.

1637 .................................................Publication of Descartes's *Discourse on Method.*

| | |
|---|---|
| 1641 | Publication of Descartes's *Meditations on First Philosophy*. |
| 1642 | Civil War begins in England; Galileo's death in his ninth year of home imprisonment. |
| 1643 | Birth of Newton. |
| 1647 | Birth of Bayle. |
| 1649 | Execution of King Charles I in England. |
| 1650 | Death of Descartes. |
| 1651 | Publication of Hobbes's *Leviathan*. |
| 1654 | Deep ties of Pascal with Jansensim; he moves to the community at Port-Royal. |
| 1660 | Restoration of the Stuart monarchy in England; Hobbes returns to favor. |
| 1662 | Death of Pascal; discovery of his notes for a defense of the Christian faith, soon published as his *Pensées*. |
| 1663 | Formation of the Royal Society in England. |
| 1666–1668 | Newton's 18 months in Woolesthorpe, changing the history of human thought. |
| 1679 | Death of Hobbes. |
| 1681 | Bayle takes refuge among French Huguenots in Rotterdam, all fleeing from persecution of Protestantism in France. |
| 1685 | Revocation of the Edict of Nantes, formally and officially ending all toleration of Protestantism in France. |

| 1687 | Publication, in Latin, of Newton's *Mathematical Principles of Natural Philosophy*. |
|------|--------|
| 1689 | Birth of Montesquieu. |
| 1690 | Publication of Locke's *Essay Concerning Human Understanding* and of his *Two Treatises of Government*. |
| 1692 | Birth of Joseph Butler. |
| 1694 | Birth of Voltaire (François-Marie Arouet). |
| 1695 | Publication of Locke's *The Reasonableness of Christianity*. |
| 1697 | Publication of the first edition of Bayle's *Historical and Critical Dictionary*, which will be frequently revised and republished. |
| 1704 | Death of Locke. |
| 1706 | Death of Bayle. |
| 1709 | Birth of La Mettrie. |
| 1711 | Birth of Hume. |
| 1712 | Birth of Rousseau. |
| 1713 | Birth of Diderot. |
| 1715 | Death of Louis XIV in France. |
| 1721 | Publication and great success of Montesquieu's *Lettres Persanes*. |
| 1726 | Publication of Butler's *Sermons on Human Nature*. |
| 1727 | Death of Newton; buried in Westminster Abbey. |
| 1734 | Publication and scandal of Voltaire's *Philosophical Letters*. |

1736 ................................................ Concerned about the growth of disbelief, Butler publishes his *Analogy of Religion, Natural and Revealed, to the Constitution and Course of Nature.*

1738 ................................................ Butler elevated to bishop in the Church of England; birth of Beccaria in Milan.

1740 ................................................ Publication of Hume's *A Treatise of Human Nature.*

1746 ................................................ Diderot becomes editor of the *Encyclopedie.*

1747 ................................................ Publication of La Mettrie's *L'Homme Machine.*

1748 ................................................ Publication of Montesquieu's *Spirit of the Laws* and of Hume's *An Enquiry Concerning Human Understanding.*

1750 ................................................ Publication of Rousseau's First "Discourse," *On the Arts and Sciences.*

1751 ................................................ Publication of Voltaire's *History of the Century of Louis XIV,* of d'Alembert's *Discours Preliminaire,* and of Hume's *An Enquiry Concerning the Principles of Morals.*

1751–1772 ...................................... Publication of the *Encyclopedie.*

1752 ................................................ Death of Butler.

1755 ................................................ Death of Montesquieu; publication of Rousseau's Second "Discourse," *On the Origins of Inequality.*

1759 ................................................ Publication of Voltaire's *Candide.*

1762 ................................................ Rousseau publishes both *Emile* and *The Social Contract*; he must flee from Paris because of his criticism of Christianity in the *Emile.*

# Glossary

**anthropomorphism**: the attribution to God of the qualities of human beings.

**anticlericalism**: the belief that the religious, social, or political influence of the clergy is harmful and should be restrained.

**apologetics**: defense by argument, most often of the Christian faith.

**Cartesian**: pertaining to Descartes or to his followers.

**corporeal**: relating to matter and to physical properties.

**deduction**: reasoning from the general to the particular or from premises to what follows logically from those premises.

**determinism**: the philosophical doctrine that all actions, including all human actions, are controlled absolutely by prior causes and are not subject either to chance or to free will.

*disputatio*: the model of teaching, examination, and argument that dominated medieval and early modern universities in Europe, based upon authority and logical deduction from received authorities.

**dualism**: the philosophical opinion that reality, and, in particular, the human being, is divided into two distinct and irreconcilable substances, body and soul.

**empiricism**: the philosophical doctrine that all knowledge arises from experience and that what cannot be confirmed by experience is not known (or naturally known).

**epistemology**: the theory or science of the origins, nature, limits, and validity of knowledge.

**essence**: the property or properties without which a thing would cease to be what it is.

**fatalism**: the belief that events are predetermined and that no human action can alter the course of things.

**fideism**: a religious form of philosophical skepticism that views the uncertainty and weakness of natural human knowledge as an indication of the necessity of faith.

**geocentric**: a system of astronomy in which the earth is the center of the cosmos.

**heliocentric**: a system of astronomy in which the sun is the center.

**hyperbolic**: excessive.

**idealism**: the philosophical doctrine that thought has as its object ideas rather than material objects.

**immutable**: not subject to or incapable of natural change.

**induction**: reasoning from the particular to the general or from a number of common facts to a general conclusion.

**Jansenism**: a movement within early modern European Catholicism that emphasized the texts of Saint Augustine that most stressed predestination and the need for personal and unmerited grace.

**Latitudinarianism**: a movement within the early modern Church of England that accepted the appropriateness of wide differences of belief, ritual, and Scriptural interpretation within Christianity.

**malleability**: the quality of being changed in form or ways of being by external influences.

**Manichean heresy**: the belief that the universe is governed by opposing and equal forces of good and evil.

**materialism**: the philosophical theory that matter is the only (or only knowable) substance in the universe.

**mechanism**: in the 17$^{th}$ and 18$^{th}$ centuries, the philosophical theory that the operations of the universe can be explained by matter-in-motion acting according to the laws of physics.

**metaphysics**: the branch of philosophy dealing with first principles and the real nature of things.

**mutable**: subject to or capable of natural change.

**naturalism**: in philosophy, the belief that there are no supernatural beings or causes in the world.

**objective being**: in Cartesian philosophy, that which is represented by an idea.

**occult force**: in certain systems of philosophy, and particularly in scholasticism, a natural cause (of a phenomenon) that is beyond the range of perception.

**ontology**: the theory or science of being and of the essence of things.

**optics**: the science of the nature and laws of light.

**Pyrrhonism**: named after the Greek skeptic Pyrrho, an extreme form of philosophical skepticism, best known for its doubt that even the proposition "Nothing can be known with certainty" could be known with certainty.

**qualitative**: pertaining to quality, and, in early modern philosophy, essence.

**quantitative**: pertaining to quantity and measurement.

**rationalism**: the philosophical doctrine that all true knowledge is found by reason alone, independent of the senses.

**relativism**: the philosophical doctrine that what we know and believe about things is relative to time, place, and circumstance.

**scholasticism**: a system of thought arising from the fusion of Aristotelian philosophy and Christian theology that dominated the schools of Europe from the late 14$^{th}$ century until the end of the 17$^{th}$ century.

**sensationalism**: the philosophical doctrine that all ideas (or all knowledge) are acquired by means of the senses.

**skepticism**: the philosophical theory that nothing can be known with certainty.

**substance**: the stuff or material of which a thing is made.

*tabula rasa*: a blank slate (the Lockean view of the human mind at birth).

**teleology**: the theory or science of "final causes," that is, of purposes or ends served.

**theodicy**: philosophical justification of God's goodness (and justice) in spite of the existence of evil and suffering.

**utility**: the moral criterion of the effect of actions or things upon human happiness (and the reduction of suffering).

# Biographical Notes

**Francis Bacon** (1561–1626). Statesman and philosopher, Bacon undertook a fundamental revision of human inquiry and knowledge. The son of a powerful Tudor politician, Bacon studied at Trinity College, Cambridge, became a barrister, and rose to the position of Lord Chancellor of the kingdom, becoming the Baron Verulam and the Viscount of St. Albans. He was dismissed from power in 1621 for bribery, a common charge in the perilous world of Tudor-Stuart politics, and he spent the final years of his life working on his great philosophical project, the *Instauratio Magna*, of which one vital part, the *Novum Organum* became his most influential legacy.

**Pierre Bayle** (1647–1706). Erudite scholar, religious controversialist, and ardent Huguenot (French Calvinist), Bayle shook the learned world of the late 17th century with his critique of intellectual arrogance, superstition, and religious intolerance. After a brief conversion to Catholicism, Bayle returned to his Calvinist origins and taught philosophy at the Protestant Academy of Sedan. He also taught philosophy and history to the growing number of persecuted Huguenots who took refuge there. Bayle feuded with the Huguenot leader, Pierre Jurieu, on matters of political theology, and he was stripped of his professorship in 1693. He served as editor a leading journal of the European learned world, wrote major works on tolerance and on religious belief, and authored a celebrated *Dictionnaire historique et critique* (1697, the first of many editions).

**Cesare Beccaria** (1738–1794). A Milanese reformist nobleman, Beccaria, at the age of 26, wrote *On Crimes and Punishments* (1764), one of the most influential texts of the European Enlightenment. Beccaria was part of an intellectual society in Milan that read authors of the French Enlightenment and that worked on plans of fiscal, administrative, and legal reform in northern Italy. *On Crimes and Punishments* earned Beccaria international fame. The work was translated into French (selling seven editions in the first six months), German, Dutch, Polish, Spanish, and English (in which form it deeply influenced Jeremy Bentham and the philosophical radicals). Beccaria remained a public official until his death, concerned with issues of economics and education, and holding a chair in Public Economy at the Palatine School in Milan.

**Joseph Butler** (1690–1752). Bishop of the Church of England, confessor and preacher at the royal court, and an admired preacher, Butler was one of the foremost moral philosophers of his age. His "Sermons on Human Nature," given at the Rolls Chapel in London, were of great influence in shaping 18$^{th}$-century discussion of nature and ethics. Increasingly concerned with Deistic unbelief, Butler published an immensely popular defense of Christianity in 1736, *The Analogy of Religion, Natural and Revealed, to the Constitution and Course of Nature.* Butler's ecclesiastic career was a series of successes: head chaplain to Caroline, the wife of King George II; bishop of Bristol; and bishop of Durham, after declining the offer of the primacy of the Church of England.

**René Descartes** (1596–1650). Descartes became the most influential Continental philosopher of the 17$^{th}$ century. Between 1618 and 1628, he travelled and studied throughout Europe while on military service, writing and publishing foundational works of mathematics and philosophy. In 1628, he moved to Holland, where censorship was far less severe than in his native France. He visited Paris in 1647 and 1648, however, meeting leading European philosophers of his age. A series of works published between 1637 and 1649—the *Discourse on Method*, the *Meditations on First Philosophy*, the *Principles of Philosophy*, and the *Treatise on the Passions*—earned him ardent disciples, and his system of philosophy soon challenged Aristotle's for dominance among European thinkers. Posthumously-published works only added to his fame. He was attacked bitterly for his challenges to the Aristotelian system, but his defenders and acolytes included both eminent theologians and eminent natural philosophers.

**Denis Diderot** (1713–1784). The son of a provincial artisan who came to Paris to study theology, Diderot became the foremost materialistic and atheistic thinker of the 18$^{th}$ century. He was best known, however, as the editor of the extraordinary publishing accomplishment of his age, the *Encyclopedie*, on which he worked from 1745 until 1772. He was a prolific author, writing novels (some quite experimental), art criticism, theater, natural philosophy, science, political theory, and a remarkably wide range of essays. In 1773, he received the patronage of Catherine the Great, Empress of Russia, who purchased his library and appointed him its librarian with an annual salary for life. After his death, the wide range of his interests became apparent from posthumous publications, and his reputation has grown steadily ever since.

**Galileo Galilei** (1564–1642). Mathematician, astronomer, inventor, and physicist, Galileo both laid the foundations of the scientific revolution of the 17th century and polemicized with astute effectiveness against the prevailing Aristotelian scholastic philosophy. In 1589, he became a lecturer in mathematics at the University of Pisa, and in 1592 he was awarded a chair in mathematics at the University of Padua, a position that he held for eighteen years. His development of an effective astronomical telescope in 1609 and his telescopic discoveries, published in 1610, made him a European celebrity. An early defender of the Copernican heliocentric theory, he was charged with heresy and theological error in 1633, forced to recant his Copernicanism, and placed under house arrest on his own estate, where he died in 1642. Although forbidden from writing during his arrest, he completed and smuggled out to the public his foundational work on the new physics.

**Thomas Hobbes** (1588–1679). An Oxford graduate who became private tutor to the powerful Cavendish family, Hobbes elaborated a complex, controversial, and widely influential system of philosophy that embraced knowledge, physics, human nature, politics, and the state. Leading the sons of the Cavendish family on the "Grand Tour" of the Continent, Hobbes had conversations with Galileo and with leading Cartesians. He published three works of central philosophical importance between 1642 and 1658, *De Corpore* (*On Body*), *De Homine* (*On Man*), and *De Cive* (*On Society*), the last of which grew into his monumental work of political philosophy, the *Leviathan*. Although his views on determinism and materialism earned him great enmity from the Church, his friendship with King Charles II (whose mathematics tutor he had been during the exile of the royal court in France during the English civil war) secured his safety. Nonetheless, after the House of Commons began investigating him in 1666, he ceased writing on human nature and devoted himself to translations from the Greek.

**David Hume** (1711–1776). Educated at the University of Edinburgh in his native Scotland, Hume became one of Europe's most influential, controversial, and revered philosophers. During an extended stay in France from 1734 to 1737, he wrote his *A Treatise of Human Nature*, which was published upon his return to Britain in 1739–1740. Its reception disappointed Hume, and his systematic views did not receive the deep attention of his age until the publication of his *An Enquiry Concerning Human Understanding* in 1748. His *Enquiry Concerning the Principles of Morals* (1751) also earned him celebrity. Suspicions about Hume's views

©1998 The Teaching Company.

on religion prevented him from obtaining the expected Chair of Moral Philosophy at Edinburgh, but he was made Keeper of the Advocates Library at Edinburgh, and, from 1763 to 1766, he served as secretary to the British Embassy in Paris, where he became a welcome participant in French intellectual and salon life. He devoted himself increasingly to history in his later years, publishing a deeply influential *History of England.* He spent the final ten years of his life among friends and admirers in Edinburgh.

**Johannes Kepler** (1571–1630). Astronomer, astrologer, mathematician, and mystic, Kepler altered the history of Western science. A student of theology and astronomy at the University of Tubingen, he joined Tycho Brahe's astronomical researchers in 1600, near Prague, under the patronage of the Holy Roman Emperor. After Brahe's death in 1601, Kepler was named Imperial Mathematician. Heir to Brahe's astronomical data, Kepler became convinced that the sun must be at the center of the system, and he deduced his three laws of planetary notion. He published extensively on the Copernican astronomy and on his own laws. Seeking greater freedom to write, he established his own printing press in Silesia in 1628. His work was essential to the Newtonian synthesis of the late 17$^{th}$ century.

**Julien Offroy de La Mettrie** (1709–1751). Controversialist, naturalist, and philosopher, La Mettrie was persecuted both for his views of the French medical profession and for his anti-spiritualist philosophy. He studied at the University of Leiden with the great life-scientist Herman Boerhaave, some of whose works he translated for the French public. He served as a surgeon to the French army. Deeply dissatisfied with the "science of man" as he found it, he undertook in a series of works to ground both medicine and theories of human nature in a naturalistic materialism, writing of mind, will, and happiness without reference to an immaterial soul. Forced to flee France, he found temporary refuge in Holland, but he was called in 1748 to the court of Frederick the Great of Prussia, where he was appointed to the Academy of Science in Berlin. He died of ptomaine poisoning at Frederick's court, giving rise in France to the story that he killed himself by his materialistic gluttony. An edition of his works was published very shortly after his death.

**John Locke** (1632–1704). A foundational thinker in modern theories of epistemology, political philosophy, education, scriptural interpretation, and religious toleration, Locke was educated at Christ Church College, Oxford, where he was early interested in the new experimental sciences. He spent a great deal of time abroad, first on diplomatic missions, then during a four-year stay in France (where he furthered his interest in the new empirical sciences), and finally in Holland during a difficult political period from 1683 until 1689. He returned to England in 1689, a leading political theorist of the Glorious Revolution of 1688. Locke was and is best known for his *Essay Concerning Human Understanding*, *Second Treatise on Government*, *The Reasonableness of Christianity*, and *A Third Letter Concerning Toleration.*

**Charles-Louis de Secondat, baron de Montesquieu** (1689–1755). Son and heir of an aristocratic family of the *parlement* de Bordeaux (the supreme provincial law court), and educated first by the Oratorians and then in the Law, Montesquieu became one of the most influential and widely read political theorists of the 18th century, with an international influence. Participating early in the academies of Bordeaux and then in the *Academie Francaise*, Montesquieu came to prominence with his satiric and probing *Lettres Persanes* in 1721, a work on the greatness and decline of Rome, published in 1734, and his pathbreaking work *L'Esprit des loix* (*The Spirit of the Laws*) in 1748, a book that earned him the widest range of criticism and admiration and that many believe lay the foundation of sociological thinking.

**Isaac Newton** (1643–1727). Originally destined to follow his father into commercial farming, Newton distinguished himself at Trinity College, Cambridge University, and he became the foremost scientific mind of the early modern era. When Cambridge was closed because of the plague, in 1666–1668, Newton returned to Woolesthorpe, in Lincolnshire, where, in eighteen months, he developed the foundations of the calculus, derived the inverse square law upon which the theory of gravitation would be based, derived his laws of motion and of planetary motion, and developed the modern theory of light. In 1669, he became Lucasian professor of mathematics at Trinity College, keeping almost all of his other discoveries to himself. His theory of the world, *The Mathematical Principles of Natural Philosophy*, was published in Latin in 1687 (translated into English in 1729), and his *Opticks* in 1704. He was knighted for his contributions to knowledge, and he was buried in Westminster Abbey.

**Blaise Pascal** (1623–1662). A child prodigy in mathematics, Pascal abandoned, with periods of activity interspersed, a breathtaking scientific career as a young man to devote himself primarily to the religious life, including religious controversies and apologetics. In mathematics and science, he won international acclaim for his work on cycloid curves,

©1998 The Teaching Company.

barometrics, geometry, and hydrodynamics, and the mechanics of calculation. After an intense conversion to Jansenism, he lived a generally ascetic and devout life, writing an immensely successful Augustinian criticism of Jesuit casuistry, *Les Provinciales* (*The Provincial Letters*), and an unfinished apologia of Christianity, published posthumously as his *Pensées*, a work of immediate and enduring influence and popularity.

**Jean-Jacques Rousseau** (1712–1778). A self-educated refugee in France from Geneva (from which he fled an unhappy apprenticeship to an engraver), Rousseau became one of the most beloved and one of the most hated thinkers of the 18th century, and a thinker of immediate and ongoing importance. In Paris from the 1740s until 1756, he moved in Enlightenment circles, but he offered foundational criticism of the *philosophes'* belief in progress and what he saw as their overreliance upon reason. From 1756 to 1761, he lived outside of Paris, writing a variety of genres with great success. In 1762, the year that his influential works *Emile* and *The Social Contract* were published, he was banished from Paris for his criticisms of Christianity in the *Emile*, and he fled to Switzerland where he was the subject of Protestant persecution. He spent an unhappy stretch in England, returning to France in 1767, and composing major works of self-examination, including his celebrated *Confessions*.

**Voltaire** [François-Marie Arouet] (1694–1778). Educated by the Jesuits and destined by his father for an administrative career, Voltaire became the most prolific and influential of all authors of the French Enlightenment. He earned early celebrity as a poet and dramatist, spent a period of exile in England (writing the *Philosophical Letters*, published in 1734), and became internationally renowned for (in addition to his theater and poetry) his histories, didactic and mordant philosophical tales, popularizations of natural philosophy and science, criticism, and, with most influence, his campaign on behalf of religious toleration. The *Philosophical Letters* led to his banishment from Paris, and he worked from 1734 until 1749 at Cirey, with Madame du Chatelet, writing above all on science, history, and religion. At the invitation of Frederick the Great, he spent a few unhappy years at the Prussian court, and settled eventually on an estate at Ferney that straddled the French and Genevan borders. There, he wrote prolifically, intensifying his campaign for toleration, and he aided young Enlightenment authors. Ferney became a kind of intellectual court for the learned and even, at times, for the powerful. He was received and feted in 1778 in Paris, his banishment having been lifted, and he died in the midst of great official and unofficial celebrations in his honor. Perhaps more than even has been the case with any other author, his pen actually may have been mightier than most swords.

# Bibliography

**Essential Reading:**

d'Alembert, Jean le Rond, *Preliminary Discourse to the Encyclopedia of Diderot*. Translated by Richard N. Schwab, with the collaboration of Walter Rex. Indianapolis: Bobbs-Merrill, 1963. This work is a window into the mind of the Enlightenment just as the movement begins to comes of consciousness of itself.

Aristotle, *Metaphysics*. Edited and translated by Richard Hope. Ann Arbor: University of Michigan Press, 1960. This is an outstanding translation (first published by Columbia University Press in 1952) of the essential Aristotelian work, and it includes appropriate selections from Aristotle's *Physics* in helpful sequence.

Bacon, Francis, *Novum Organum*. Translated and edited by Peter Urbach and John Gibson. Chicago: Open Court, 1994. In Bacon's "Introduction" and in Book One, you will find his clearest presentation of his vast project for a new knowledge. The later 17th century was deeply inspired and influenced by this work, and the 17th and 18th centuries are almost incomprehensible without a familiarity with the vision offered in this work.

Bayle, Pierre, *Historical and Critical Dictionary*. Translated and edited by Richard H. Popkin. Indianapolis: Hackett, 1985. Bayle's *Dictionary* was of monumental importance in the history of philosophy and critical erudition. The selection here illuminates Bayle's sense of the conflict between faith and reason when reason addresses areas beyond its ken, and it includes Bayle's important "Clarifications" in which he defends himself against charges of impiety and indecency.

Beccaria, Cesare, *On Crimes and Punishments, and other writings*. Edited by Richard Bellamy. Translated by Richard Davies, with Virginia Cox and Richard Bellamy. Cambridge and New York: Cambridge University Press, 1995. In addition to the text of its central work, which influenced European and American legal reform for more than two generations, this edition includes important works included in the French translation of 1766 and other works that illustrate Beccaria's broader Enlightenment concerns.

Butler, Joseph, *Five Sermons, Preached at the Rolls Chapel and A Dissertation upon the Nature of Virtue*. Edited by Stephen L. Darwall. Indianapolis: Hackett, 1983. Bishop Butler's sermons on human nature were simultaneously broadly representative of the naturalizing tendency within Anglican moral theology in the 18th century and exceptionally influential in forming a Christian school of moral theology that stressed the providential harmony of happiness and virtue.

Descartes, René, *Meditations on First Philosophy.* Edited and translated by John Cottingham. Revised edition. New York: Cambridge University Press, 1996. This is an excellent edition of Descartes's immensely influential and controversial work of fundamental metaphysics, and it includes the "Objections and Replies" published in the first 17th-century edition, which permits the reader to understand how Descartes was read (and objected to) in his own lifetime and how he defended his positions.

_____. *The Passions of the Soul.* Translated by Stephen Voss. Indianapolis: Hackett, 1989. This work reveals how far Descartes goes in explaining human phenomena physiologically and mechanistically, and, though vital, how minimal a role he assigns to any immaterial agency in man. It is important to read *The Passions of the Soul* with the *Meditations*, in order to have a full sense of the Cartesian agenda.

Diderot, Denis, *D'Alembert's Dream,* in *Rameau's Nephew/D'Alembert's Dream.* Translated by Leonard Tancock. London: Penguin Books, 1966. This is Diderot's most speculative work, in which he extends the boundaries of naturalistic explanation as far as he can (literally) imagine. You should read it as speculative work, not as a scientific opus, despite its evolutionary theories and its anticipation of genetic replication. Diderot is imagining what form explanations without God or spirit might take; he is not writing from scientific knowledge. His moral speculations in the third dialogue are among the frankest of the Enlightenment.

Galileo, *Discoveries and Opinions of Galileo.* Translated and edited by Stillman Drake. New York: Anchor Books, 1957. This is an important and historically dramatic compilation of major works by Galileo, accomplished by Stillman Drake, one of the century's most eminent scholars and translators of Galileo's works. It includes, among other works, *The Starry Messenger*, in which Galileo announced some of his most startling discoveries (since he perfected the astronomical telescope), the *Letter to the Grand Duchess Christina*, in which he articulated his profoundly influential views of the relationship between science and scripture, and a significant excerpt from *The Assayer*, in which he attacks, with verve, the natural philosophy of the Aristotelians. Drake links them together with an interesting narrative. Reading these pieces, one encounters not merely the scientific and philosophical Galileo, but also the bitterly anti-Aristotelian intellectual brawler.

Hobbes, Thomas, *Leviathan*. Edited by C.B. Macpherson. London: Penguin Books, 1985. This work is not only one of the great classics of political theory, but, more deeply, an entire philosophical project based upon a theory of knowledge, human nature, and human motivation. Everyone reads the political theory of Book II; you should read, above all, the theory of human nature in Book I and the reflections on religion, philosophy, and politics in Books III and IV.

Hume, David, *Dialogues Concerning Natural Religion and the Posthumous Essays*. Edited by Richard H. Popkin. Indianapolis: Hackett, 1980. Hume's *Dialogues*, published posthumously in the 18th century, were and are a remarkable exploration and examination of the arguments for and against the claim that we know of God from the study of nature by the natural human faculties. This edition includes two essays that Hume withheld from his earlier philosophical works, "Of the Immortality of the Soul," and "Of Suicide," that also critically examine deeply held Christian beliefs.

Kors, Alan Charles and Paul Korshin, editors, *Anticipations of the Enlightenment in England, France, and Germany*. In this work an international group of authors argues that so much of what historians generally attribute to the mid to late 18th century was present in the intellectual life of the generation from 1680 to 1715.

Koyre, Alexandre, *Newtonian Studies*. Cambridge, Mass.: Harvard University Press, 1965. Koyre was a singularly deep, astute, and influential scholar, with a remarkable sense both of Newton's mind and method, on the one hand, and of Newton's relationship to the long-term history of Western philosophy and religion, on the other.

La Mettrie, Julien Offray de, *Machine Man and Other Writings*. Translated and edited by Ann Thomson. Cambridge and New York: Cambridge University Press, 1996. There has been a recent flurry of critical editions of La Mettrie's works, including an important work by Thomson herself, but this is by far the best and most welcome compilation of La Mettrie's thought, offering not only *Machine Man*, but other works on the human being, on ethics, on the Stoics and Epicureans, and on philosophy in general.

Locke, John, *An Essay Concerning Human Understanding*. Abridged and edited by A.D. Woozley. New York: Meridian, 1974. Locke's *Essay* dominated Western notions of knowledge for a century, and understanding the *Essay* is essential for understanding both the 17th and 18th centuries.

Woozley's abridgement does justice to Locke's essential arguments and language.

Montesquieu, Charles de Secondat, baron de, *The Persian Letters.* Translated by C.J. Betts. London: Penguin Books, 1973. This is a superb translation of Montesquieu's exotic, philosophical, best-selling work, one of the true publishing sensations of the 18th century. It exposes the reader not only to Montesquieu's quest for universals among the relativistic beliefs and practices of mankind, but to his wit and social criticism.

Newton, Isaac., *Newton's Philosophy of Nature*: *Selections from His Writings.* Edited by H.S. Thayer. New York: Hafner, 1953. This excellent anthology of Newton's writings exposes the readers to the heart of his discoveries, and his views of method, hypothesis, experiment, mathematical reasoning, and God in natural philosophy. It also includes the preface by Cotes to the first English edition of Newton's *Principia*, which demonstrates how Newton's thought was explained and popularized.

Pascal, Blaise, *Pensées.* Translated by A.J. Krailsheimer. London: Penguin Books, 1966. Despite Pascal's often marginalized place in 17th-century religious debates, being a Jansenist in revolt against the worldliness of other forms of Catholicism, the *Pensées* were an instant best-seller in France, beloved across a wide spectrum of beliefs, and they have stood as one of the most influential religious writings of Western civilization.

Pocock, J.G.A., *Politics, Language, and Time.* Revised edition. Chicago: University of Chicago Press, 1989. Almost every essay in this volume in a gem, including the self-criticism added in 1989, but the first essay, "Languages and their Implication," although it uses the history of political thought as its subject, is a magisterial lesson on the nature of an empirical and contextual intellectual history, on the multivalence of ideas, and on the study of fundamental change in human thought.

Rousseau, Jean-Jacques. *The Social Contract and Discourse on the Origin of Inequality.* Edited by Lester G. Crocker. New York: Simon and Schuster, 1967. This edition uses an excellent (and anonymous) 1761 English translation of the *Discours* and the superb Henry J. Tozer 19th-century translation of the *Contrat Social.* The *Discourse* establishes Rousseau's view of the catastrophic cost that we have paid for civilization, and *The Social Contract* offers one of Rousseau's senses of how we might repair a major portion of that damage. It is enlightening, thus, to read the two works together.

Tindal, Matthew, *Christianity as Old as the Creation.* Stuttgart: Friedrich Frommann, 1957. This is a facsimile publication of the 1730 edition of Tindal's celebrated and notorious work, termed "The Bible of Deism" by opponents and admirers. Tindal's work struck a nerve, eliciting more than a hundred refutations and inspiring a generation of freethinkers.

Voltaire, *Candide and Other Writings.* Edited by Haskell M. Block. New York: Random House [The Modern Library], 1956. Using a variety of excellent translations, many of them improved by Haskell Block, this is a rich compilation of a great diversity of Voltaire's writings. It will permit the reader to experience Voltaire's pen in many genres, and where it excerpts works, it does so well.

_____. *Philosophical Letters.* Translated by Ernest Dilworth. New York: Macmillan, 1961. The great early 20th-century scholar Gustave Lanson termed this work the opening round of the French Revolution (two generations later). It should be read in its entirety, giving the reader rich exposure to the thought of the still young Voltaire on religion, politics, society, literature, and the world of learning. It had an electric effect in France, where it was a *cause célèbre* and the occasion of Voltaire's virtually lifelong banishment from Paris.

Waring, E. Graham, editor, *Deism and Natural Religion: A Source Book.* New York: F. Ungar, 1967. This outstanding anthology offers both sides of the "deist controversies" in England. It includes significant excerpts from deists, Christian natural religionists, and Christian defenders of supernatural faith against the deists. It truly exposes the reader to the broadest range of English deistic and Christian debate about the place of nature and reason in religion.

**Supplementary Reading:**

Aristotle, *Physica.* Translated by R.P. Hardie and R.K. Gaye. Volume II of *The Works of Aristotle.* Edited by W.D. Ross. Oxford: Oxford University Press, 1930. To understand fully the revolution in 17th-century notions of physics and nature, one must understand the foundation of the system against which the new philosophy directed its criticisms; this was that foundation.

Bacon, Francis, *The Complete Essays of Francis Bacon, Including The New Atlantis. Edited by Henry LeRoy Finch.* New York: Washington Square Press, 1963. This work provides the reader not only with Bacon's visionary *The New Atlantis*, in which he offers a utopian view of a society organized around the charitable use of a new human knowledge derived from a new experimental science, but also his *Essays or Counsels Civil and Moral*, which offer much insight into the more worldly thinking of this Elizabethan and Tudor statesman.

Betts, C.J., *Early Deism in France. From the so-called 'deistes' of Lyon (1564) to Voltaire's 'Lettres Philosophiques' (1734).* The Hague and Boston: Martinus Nijhoff, 1984. This is a learned and interesting history of the emergence of anti-Christian deistic thinking in France, with an excellent bibliography.

Chastellux, François-Jean, *An Essay on Public Happiness.* 2 vols. New York: A.M. Kelley, 1969. This is a reprint of the 1774 English translation of this classic work, first published, in French, in 1770. Voltaire (perhaps in a moment of weakness) called this book "greater than Montesquieu's *Spirit of the Laws*), which may not be the judgment of posterity, but which tells us something of Chastellux's place in the 18th century. The book is a window onto the thinking of the French Enlightenment about utility, the theoretical problem of reconciling public and private happiness, and the role of the Church in society.

Descartes, René, *Discourse on Method.* There are scores of editions and translations of this profoundly influential work, a discourse that altered the course of the 17th century and, indeed, of European philosophy. Read any unabridged edition.

_____. *Treatise of Man.* French text with translation by Thomas Steele Hall. Cambridge, Mass: Harvard University Press, 1972. This work deeply influenced the thought of the second half of the 17th century and did much to bridge the "scientific" and the "philosophical" study of human beings.

Galileo, *Dialogue Concerning the Two Chief World Systems–Ptolemaic and Copernican.* Translated by Stillman Drake. Forward by Albert Einstein. Second edition. Berkeley: University of California Press, 1970. In theory, this was Galileo's neutral exposition of the two great systems; in fact, it was a sustained polemical and scientific work on behalf of the Copernican system. Although many of its arguments on behalf of Copernicus did not survive scrutiny, its refutation of the Ptolemaic and scholastic astronomy was profoundly effective and influential.

Gay, Peter, editor, *Deism: An Anthology.* New York: Van Nostrand, 1968. This compilation offers examples of deistic writing from deism's precursors in the 17th century to deism's flowering in England, on the continent, and in America in the 18th century. Unlike Waring's anthology (see above), the reader is not exposed to Christian replies, but Gay's anthology offers a more geographically and intellectually broad sampling of deistic authors.

Haakonssen, Knud, *Natural Law and Moral Philosophy from Grotius to the Scottish Enlightenment*. Cambridge and New York: Cambridge University Press, 1996. This is a quite stunning analytic survey of the development of thinking about natural law in moral philosophy, with a broad scope, many compelling individual discussions, and a rich bibliography.

Halevy, Elie, *The Growth of Philosophic Radicalism*. Translated by May Morries. Boston: Beacon Press, 1966. This is a classic study of utilitarianism: its birth in the 18th century and its adoption by English reformers in the late 18th and in the 19th centuries. It understands the central role of French Enlightenment works in this development. This work, first published in French earlier in the century, has become a touchstone for almost all later work on utilitarianism.

Hazard, Paul, *The European Mind, 1680–1715*. New York: World Publishing, 1963. First published, in French, in 1935 (under the title *La crise de la conscience européenne, 1690–1715*, a more dramatic title than in its English translation), Hazard's work is a classic and a common point of reference for all later historians.

Hobbes, Thomas, *Metaphysical Writings*. Edited by Mary Whiton Calkins. New edition. Chicago: Open Court, 1989. This is an outstanding compilation of major excerpts from Hobbes's *Elements of Philosophy Concerning Body* and from his treatise on *Human Nature*, and will permit the reader to situate the project of the *Leviathan* in the context of Hobbes's broader philosophical concerns.

Hume, David, *Writings on Religion*. Edited by Antony Flew. Chicago: Open Court, 1992. This is an outstanding compilation of Hume's scattered writing on religion, and it includes his crucial work *A Natural History of Religion*. Flew is a first-rate philosopher, and he adds astute observations.

Kors, Alan Charles, *Atheism in France, 1650–1729: The Orthodox Sources of Disbelief*. Princeton: Princeton University Press, 1990. The opening chapters lay out an agenda for a contextual intellectual history. A later section, "The Fratricide," focuses on the intensity of Aristotelian-Cartesian debate.

_____. "The Atheism of d'Holbach and Naigeon," in Michael Hunter and David Wootton, editors, *Atheism from the Reformation to the Enlightenment*. Oxford and New York: Oxford University Press, 1992, pp. 273–300. A presentation of the origins and nature of the materialistic thought of two thinkers who went beyond their friend Diderot in proselytism for atheism.

Koyre, Alexandre, *Metaphysics and Measurement: Essays in Scientific Revolution.* Cambridge, Mass.: Harvard University Press, 1968. For students wishing to understand the central role of the new mathematics and philosophy of quantification in the scientific revolution of the 17th century, there is no more provocative, concise book.

Locke, John, *The Reasonableness of Christianity with A Discourse of Miracles and part of A Third Letter Concerning Toleration.* Edited and abridged by I.T. Ramsey. Stanford: Stanford University Press, 1958. Locke's *Reasonableness* was simultaneously an expression of the new naturalizing tendencies of Christianity under the influence of the new philosophy, one of the most extreme examples of that tendency, and, given Locke's immense philosophical prestige, one of the most widely-debated such works. The letter on toleration, with its notion of the voluntary nature of a church, was and is a landmark in Western thinking about civil tolerance.

Leibniz, Gottfried Wilhelm, *Theodicy: Essays on the Goodness of God, the Freedom of Man, and the Origin of Evil.* Leibniz's work, so ferociously satirized in Voltaire's *Candide*, is a powerful work of natural philosophy that lay at the heart of so much of 18th-century philosophical and theological optimism. To understand the crisis in confidence of the mid-18th century, one should understand the height of that confidence in its earlier forms.

Montesquieu, Charles de Secondat, baron de, *The Spirit of the Laws.* Translated and edited by Anne M. Cohler, Basia Carolyn Miller, and Harold Samuel Stone. Cambridge and New York: Cambridge University Press, 1989. This work was profoundly influential in the 18th century, and, in many minds, set the foundations of Western comparative thinking about societies across geography and time. One should not leave the 18th century without reading it.

Newton, Isaac, *The Mathematical Principles of Natural Philosophy.* Translated and edited by Florian Cajori. 2 vols. Berkeley: University of California Press, 1934. This superb edition, now in paperback, is the ultimate source for Newton's natural philosophy and for the watershed accomplishment of the 17th century's revolution in science and method. The mathematics remain daunting, but the reader will encounter the birth of a model of thinking about nature that would dominate the following centuries.

Pascal, Blaise, *The Provincial Letters*. Translated by J. Krailsheimer. Baltimore: Penguin Books, 1967. Pascal's mordant and blistering attack on what he took be the moral theology of Jesuit casuistry was one of the most successful polemical works of the 17th century. For the reader, it is a captivating window onto Jansenist thought in general, and into the passions of the 17th century on issues of sin and grace in particular.

Rex, Walter, *Essays on Pierre Bayle and Religious Controversy*. The Hague: M. Nijhoff, 1965. This is the best book on Bayle in English, and it was part of the revolution in Bayle scholarship that restored him to his Calvinist and fideistic origins. It is a book that reveals how understanding context changes the way one reads a text.

Rousseau, Jean-Jacques, *Emile*. Translated and edited by Allan Bloom. New York: Basic Books, 1979. Rousseau's seminal treatise on education established an influential view of original human nature, a "natural" education that would minimize the depredation of artificial society, and a model of learning that would follow the Lockean model of human knowledge and motivation. A section on religious education earned him official persecution.

Voltaire, *Micromegas* and the "Poem on the Lisbon Earthquake," both in *Candide and Other Writings* (see above), and both indispensable to understanding, in the first work, Voltaire's sense of the limits of human knowledge (and of human nature), and, in the second work, the Voltairean crisis that led to the writing of *Candide*.

Wade, Ira O., *The Intellectual Development of Voltaire*. Princeton: Princeton University Press, 1969. This is a magnificent study of Voltaire's intellectual development by the foremost Voltaire scholar of the 20th century. It is a classic. It is an encyclopedic work, but it is exceptionally well organized, and the reader may read selectively by interest to his or her great profit.

# Notes